Contents

KT-436-041

Introduction to Vocational Business series

This textbook is one of a series covering the core areas of business studies. The first six books in the series cover the core units of the Business AVCE. A further five books look at the most popular optional units. Each book focuses on vocational aspects of business, rather than theoretical models, allowing the reader to understand how businesses operate. To complement this vocational focus, each book contains a range of case studies illustrating how businesses respond to internal and external changes.

The textbooks are designed to support students taking a range of business courses. While each is free standing, containing the essential knowledge required by the various syllabuses and course requirements, together they provide a comprehensive coverage of the issues facing both large and small businesses in today's competitive environment.

Titles in the series

Book 1	**Business at Work**
Book 2	**The Competitive Business Environment**
Book 3	**Marketing**
Book 4	**Human Resources**
Book 5	**Finance**
Book 6	**Business Planning**
Optional units:	**Financial Accounting**
	Market Research
	Marketing and Promotional Strategy
	Training and Development
	Business and the European Union

Acknowledgements

I could not have completed this book without the support, patience and guidance from my wife, Pippa, and my children, to whom I owe a great deal. Simon Benn of The Times 100 was a continuing support and source of ideas throughout. Thanks also to Dave Needham for getting me into this, as well as the support of Nelson Thornes. Finally, I owe a great deal to the students and staff of The Priory LSST, in particular Richard Gilliland.

Darren Gelder

Great appreciation goes to my wife, Carol, and my children Katie, Phoebe and Josh who have had to put up with me writing this book for endless hours instead of paying them the attention they deserve. Thanks also to Darren Gelder, my chief supporter, who kept me going when ideas were not flowing freely (and made threats as appropriate!). Finally, thanks to Dr John Pratten from Manchester Metropolitan University, without whom I would not have been given the chance to enter the field of examinations and gain the experience necessary to enable me to contribute to this book.

Paul Woodcock

The authors and publishers would also like to thank the following people and organisations for permission to reproduce material:

The Body Shop International plc; Nestlé UK; Guardian Newspapers Limited; The Economist Newspaper Limited; Cosmopolitan Magazine; Chemical Engineering; Kenwood Marks Limited; Weetabix Limited; Orange Personal Communications Services Limited; Mars UK Limited; Kellogg Company; Bank of England; Assessment and Qualifications Alliance; OCR; and Edexcel.

Every effort has been made to contact copyright holders and we apologise if any have been overlooked.

Author profile

Darren Gelder is Head of Business Studies at The Priory LSST, Lincoln. He is senior educational advisor to The Times 100, and contributing author to *Vocational Education Magazine*. Darren is also a founder member of the Business Studies Teachers Network (BSTN), as well as being a member of the Nottingham University Business Team.

Paul Woodcock is second in department in the Business Studies department at the Priory LSST, Lincoln. He is a principal examiner for AQA for VCE Business Studies, QCA assessor for GCSE Economics and VCE Business Studies papers and has examined for OCR. He is a founder member of the Business Studies Teachers Network (BSTN) and has worked for MBA Publishing in helping to produce teacher support materials for use on the Times 100 website.

Marketing and Promotional Strategy

Introduction

How to use the book

To ensure you get the most from this book you should, wherever possible, relate the issues raised to the organisation that you have chosen to study.

Selecting an organisation

Most boards require you to base your portfolio around a business or businesses; considering how much time and work that you are going to be putting in, it is essential you make the right decision. You must ask yourself the following questions:

- Do I have access to someone in the business who can provide me with the information that I need?
- Is the organisation the right size/sector?
- What is the best way to collect the information regarding the organisation?

It is essential that time and preparation are spent on this area. Too often students get halfway through a portfolio unit and realise they can't get the rest of the information they require. A major part of any vocational course is planning; for any student to achieve well at this level they must take responsibility for their own actions.

It is advised that students draw up a plan of how they are going to tackle the unit. This could include:

- identifying **all** the information that is needed to complete the unit
- deciding and arranging how best to collect the information and when to do it
- making arrangements with organisations and individuals (dates and times)
- ensuring you have a plan of how you will put the portfolio together, driven by the assessment evidence
- identifying as soon as possible any missing areas, or gaps in either your data or your theory.

The purpose of this book is to help you meet the assessment criteria of your exam board. It will also ensure that you gain as high a mark as is possible. The book will explain clearly all the relevant information you need. It will also explain how it works and what you need to look for in your chosen organisations.

Throughout the book, areas will be highlighted that require careful attention. They will be flagged by the following headings:

Need to know and Need to do

These will highlight specific areas that you must either mention or focus on in your portfolio to ensure that you meet the evidence assessment criteria.

Need to know

There are requirements in all specifications of certain knowledge that you must have; throughout the book these will be highlighted to enable you to include them in your work. You will need to know what the principles of marketing are, therefore this must form part of your work when you discuss or relate the principles to the organisation that you are investigating.

Need to do

Again all specifications expect you to carry out certain tasks to complete your portfolio and ensure success. You will need to compare various roles or departments of an organisation and you may need to collect certain information.

It is essential that you pay particular attention to these areas.

Case material

Throughout the book reference will be made to actual case material where the topic being covered can be seen in operation. This will allow you to relate it to 'real-life' situations; it will also allow you to use the material in your portfolio. There will also be references throughout the book to useful websites – these can be used to give further information and examples or reference material.

Portfolio advice

All the boards break their grades into three distinct areas; the lower areas can be achieved by simply obtaining the information and applying it. However, the higher grades can only be achieved through evaluation and analysis. This book will give you advice on how to achieve the higher marks, but it is down to you to put it into practice.

The book will also look at the three main examining bodies: AQA, OCR and Edexcel, and give specific guidance and advice on how to meet the assessment criteria for each of them.

Planning a campaign

What is promotional planning all about?

The plan

When considering the planning of a promotional campaign it is important from the outset to have a clear understanding of what a plan is and what use it has to the management of the promotional campaign.

A plan is simply a design for achieving a specific objective (or several specific objectives).

 Objectives, page 7

The plan can relate to any time period, and the longer the time period the less specific the objective can be. It is therefore vital when putting a plan together that you are aware of the timescale involved. For instance, if the objective is to see 80 per cent awareness of a product nationally, the promotion plan to achieve that within four weeks will be far more aggressive and involved than a plan to achieve 80 per cent awareness within two years.

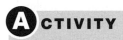 CTIVITY

Task 1

Write down five areas of your own life where a plan would help you achieve your goal, for instance a revision plan for a forthcoming external unit test.

Task 2

Take one of your areas and identify three benefits that you would derive as a result of your plan. For instance, a revision plan would benefit you because you would ensure that all important areas in the unit have been covered, enabling you to have sufficient knowledge to at least attempt any questions on those areas.

The process

Promotional planning is the planned application of marketing resources to achieve sales promotion objectives. The planning aspect of the campaign is a process that begins with the manager of the campaign determining a systematic way of identifying a range of options, selecting those which are necessary and then producing a schedule with costings to ensure that the stated objectives are achieved. This process is never easy as each campaign will bring with it its own problems, needs and constraints and all of these must be considered before arriving at a final decision. One of the biggest hurdles to overcome is deciding on a compromise between what is desirable and what is practicable, and it is here that the success or failure of a campaign is often decided.

This problem will be covered in detail when we look at the factors necessary for objectives to be meaningful.

▶ Internal and external influences, page 41

▶ Contingency plan, page 17

Why is promotional planning essential?

Before looking in detail at how to set useful and meaningful objectives, it is important that you consider why promotional planning is essential.

With the onset of globalisation and opening up of all markets, the market is an increasingly hostile environment, and only those businesses that keep ahead of the rest are able to survive and grow. Businesses face scores of external and internal factors which interact, often in very difficult to follow ways, and each will have a bearing on the ability of that business to achieve its major objectives. Without some system in place to break this problem down into manageable segments, those managing the business would find it almost impossible to produce coherent campaigns with any real chance of success.

Contents of a marketing plan

When putting a marketing plan together it is useful from the outset to fix in your mind the purpose of the plan. The purpose of a marketing plan is to indicate a firm's progress at a specified date and how it is going to continue to progress if no changes are made. It is normal that a plan will change, and so contingency measures should be incorporated into the plan to show how your organisation would respond to sudden changes. This built-in flexibility is essential.

One thing that is vital when putting together a good marketing plan is that it should be short on words and long on figures. Any extended reports should be included in appendices.

There is no set model that must be followed when putting together a promotions plan, as the detail needed will depend upon the type and size of business, the market it operates in and how long it has been trading. However, there are certain sections that are relevant to most situations and the summary below indicates what you should include in your plan.

Look at these three examples of what your plan should include. You need to match them with the assessment criteria to decide which one is most suitable for your assignment.

The first is taken from an American marketing and promotional strategy website and gives an overview of what they consider to be the bare minimum requirements for a marketing plan.

The essential contents of a marketing plan

Every marketing plan has to fit the needs and situation. Even so, there are standard components you just can't do without. A marketing plan should always have a situation analysis, marketing strategy, sales forecast, and expense budget.

- Situation Analysis: Normally this will include a market analysis, SWOT analysis, (strengths, weaknesses, opportunities, and threats), and a competitive analysis. The market analysis will include market forecast, segmentation, customer information, and market needs analysis.

- Marketing Strategy: This should include at least a mission statement, objectives, and focused strategy including market segment focus and product positioning.

- Sales Forecast: This would include enough detail to track sales month by month and follow up on plan-vs.-actual analysis. Normally a plan will also include specific sales by product, by region or market segment, by channels, by manager responsibilities, and other elements. The forecast alone is a bare minimum.

- Expense Budget: This ought to include enough detail to track expenses month by month and follow up on plan-vs.-actual analysis. Normally a plan will also include specific sales tactics, programs, management responsibilities, promotion, and other elements. The expense budget is a bare minimum.

Source: www.bplans.com

Are they enough?

These essential requirements above are not the ideal, just the minimum. In most cases you will begin a marketing plan with an executive summary, and you will also follow those essentials just described with a review of organisational impact, risks and contingencies, and pending issues.

Include a specific action plan

You should also remember that planning is about the results, not the plan itself. A marketing plan must be measured by the results it produces. The implementation of your plan is much more important than its brilliant ideas or massive market research. You can influence implementation by building a plan full of specific, measurable and concrete plans that can be tracked and followed up. Plan-vs-actual analysis is critical to the eventual results, and you should build it into your plan.

The second example relates to a specific promotions plan:

 Market research, page 20

Sections in a promotions plan

1 Select product or products to be included in the promotional activity/campaign.

2 Conduct primary and secondary research to determine the current state of the market for the product/products. This may involve a SWOT analysis to help determine your positioning in the market and future strategy to adopt.

3 Identify and state corporate aims and objectives for the organisation.

4 State improvements needed in the market.

 Aims and objectives, page 8

SMART, page 10

 Promotion, page 13

5 State clear SMART objectives for promotion with targets, dates, etc.

6 Decide which promotion activities will be most suited to achieve the stated objectives.

7 Decide which of the promotion activities you will include, taking into account internal and external influences and costings for each activity chosen. Influences should be clearly acknowledged and explained.

8 Prepare a set of dates/timings for each aspect of the promotions campaign including start and end dates and review dates to monitor progress.

 Evaluation, page 54

9 State criteria for evaluating the campaign/activities.

10 Prepare a contingency plan for unforeseen events and/or situations where results are less than expected.

Source: *Marketing Plans*, Malcolm H.B. McDonald, 5th ed., 2002
(Butterworth-Heinemann)

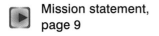
Need to know

 Mission statement, page 9

Relevance, page 11

Before continuing, a vital aspect that you must bear in mind when planning a promotional campaign is where your campaign fits into the overall aims and objectives of the business. Your promotional campaign cannot be seen in isolation from the rest of the business. The following model shows the make-up of a marketing plan and is useful as a reminder to ensure you do recognise the importance of integration of the marketing department into the business as a whole.

The third example, outlined below, gives a more comprehensive summary of the requirements of a marketing plan.

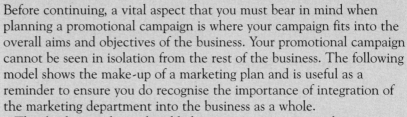

1 Subject – a brief statement of the products and main activities covered by the plan.

2 Period – states the start and end date of the plan.

3 Products – gives a detailed explanation of the products.

4 Targets – specific statements, in figures, of the quantities to be achieved for given time periods for each of the products being promoted.

5 Outline campaign plan – general overview of what you intend to do to achieve your stated targets.

6 Sales targets – a summary, mainly in table form, of sales to be achieved for each product and customer group (if relevant).

7   Market shares – a set of tables indicating market shares to be achieved for each product and, if relevant, geographical area.

8   Pricing plans – clear outline of pricing strategy and policy to be used, including discounts, for each product and stage of the campaign.

9   Promotions plan – clear specification of advertising, sales promotions and public relations campaigns, including media schedules, to be followed.

10 Influences – detailed description of competition and other influences to be accounted for including economic, social and legal.

11 Research needs – clear statement of when and how targets are to be reviewed to ensure original targets are met.

12 Finance – summary of costs of each element of the campaign.

Source: *Mastering Marketing*, Douglas Foster, 2nd ed., 1984 (Macmillan)

 Influence, page 41

Need to know

These two models can be helpful as guides to preparing your own promotional campaign and should be returned to for guidance. Whilst the first model specifically refers to a promotions model, the second model may be more relevant, depending on the specific criteria outlined for assessment in the unit specifications.

Each business will have to adapt any basic model to take account of its size, whether or not it has a diversification of products and/or markets, and what the major reason for the campaign is. However, there is one clear fact: a coordinated, consistent plan is more likely to succeed than one simply thrown together.

Need to do

The following Internet site has many examples of sample marketing and advertising plans – the one shown here relates to a large manufacturing business seeking to improve sales and market share. It would be useful to look at this sample for illustrations of how to present a full plan. The sections showing how to present budgets for different advertising activities related to stated targets are worth a look.
http://www.paloalto.com/sampleplans/protected/app4/furnituremanufacturer-app.pdf

 Evaluating, page 32

 P&G example, page 52

| Setting objectives

The initial stage of any planning process is to set a desired outcome (objective) and then communicate this to those needing to put the plan together in the department.

Hopefully, in the earlier activity when you looked at areas where plans would help your own life you were able to identify at least three benefits of having a plan. Compare your benefits with the following list.

What help are objectives to planning and decision making?

Objectives help us to:

- determine strategy
- provide a guide to action
- provide a sense of direction and unity
- provide a framework for decision making
- co-ordinate activities
- facilitate prioritisation
- measure and control performance
- encourage a concentration on long-term factors
- motivate employees.

In *Marketing Plans*, written for the Institute of Marketing, Malcolm H.B. McDonald wrote about the need for objectives in advertising, the sentiments of which apply to you in setting your promotions objectives:

We need to set objectives for advertising for the following reasons:

1 We need to set the budget for advertising. Therefore we need some objectives.

2 We need to determine who our target audience is. Therefore we need some objectives.

3 We need to determine the content of advertisements. Therefore we need some objectives.

4 We need to decide on what media to use. Therefore we need some objectives.

5 We need too decide on the frequency of advertising. Therefore we need some objectives.

6 We need to decide on how to measure the effectiveness of our advertising. Therefore we need some objectives.

How are objectives presented?

There are two mnemonics which help when looking at the different types of objective and the setting of useful, meaningful and relevant objectives.

MOST

Firstly, there is a hierarchy of objectives summarised by the mnemonic 'MOST'. The initial letters indicate the hierarchy of objectives:

- **M**ission statement – this indicates the purpose and direction of the business.
- **O**bjectives – these are the long-term goals of the business.
- **S**trategy – this refers to the long-term plan designed to achieve the mission and objectives.
- **T**actics – these are the short-term plans for implementing the strategies. The mission statement and corporate objectives detail what an organisation is seeking to achieve, the strategy and tactics detail how an organisation will achieve it.

 Attracting new customers, page 15

ⒸASE STUDY

The Body Shop mission statement

Our Reason for Being

The Body Shop International plc – a company with a difference.

- To dedicate our business to the pursuit of social and environmental change.
- To creatively balance the financial and human needs of our stakeholders: employees, customers, franchisees, suppliers and shareholders.
- To courageously ensure that our business is ecologically sustainable: meeting the needs of the present without compromising the future.
- To meaningfully contribute to local, national and international communities in which we trade, by adopting a code of conduct which ensures care, honesty, fairness and respect.
- To passionately campaign for the protection of the environment, human and civil rights, and against animal testing within the cosmetics and toiletries industry.
- To tirelessly work to narrow the gap between principle and practice, whilst making fun, passion and care part of our daily lives.

Further information about The Body Shop can be found on their website at: www.thebodyshop.com

© 2002 The Body Shop International plc

ⒶCTIVITY

Tasks

1 Read the mission statement for The Body Shop above and summarise in one sentence what you believe is The Body Shop's reason for existence.

2 From your own experience of The Body Shop, using marks out of ten, how successful would you rank their achievement of their main aims? Explain why you gave this score, providing at least two reasons to support your answer.

Figure 1 A strategy pyramid

The figure above shows a basic **strategy pyramid** for marketing plans, highlighting three of the four elements of the mnemonic MOST.

Strategy, at the top of the pyramid, is a matter of focusing on specific markets, market needs, and product or service offerings. Tactics, in the middle level, set the marketing message and the way it should be transmitted. Programs, at the base of the pyramid, provide the specifics of implementation.

The pyramid emphasises the practical importance of building a solid marketing plan structure. Most marketing plans are developed from the top-level – strategy first. Tactics follow strategy. The foundation, of course, is built on specific programs with their specific milestone dates, expense budgets, and projected sales results.

SMART

All objectives, whether short or long term, in order to be worthwhile, need to be 'SMART'.

SMART is a mnemonic which represents the desirable features of objectives and stands for:

- Specific
- Measurable
- Achievable
- Relevant/Realistic
- Time constrained.

Taking each in turn:

Specific

Any objective must be specific. It is no point setting an objective of 'improving sales', as selling one item more than the previous month would achieve this objective. However, if the marketing team were looking for a three per cent increase, then that would be a specific objective that could be targeted by the marketing team.

Measurable

All objectives need to be measurable. This enables clear planning to take place and also evaluation of the campaign to be made by comparing the results with the objective. A measurable objective would quantify what was being aimed for, for instance, increased sales revenue of £2000, increased sales of 200 units.

Achievable

Not only should objectives be specific and measurable, they should also be achievable.

It may sound really optimistic to state that your objective with a sales campaign is to capture 50 per cent of the market share by the end of the year; if this is related to the launch of a new chocolate snack product where the main brands are Kit Kat, Twix and Mars bars, your objective is likely to be highly unachievable within a 12-month period, if ever! Unachievable objectives can be demotivating, and in an industry where salary is often related to achieving stated objectives, such demotivation could also lead to high staff turnover and poor corporate image.

Relevant

Objectives should always be set in line with the achievement of the business's overall aims. This aspect is vital, otherwise a promotional campaign, though successful in achieving the stated objectives, may impede the progress of the business. For example, if a business plans to stop selling a particular brand because its corporate aims include concentrating only on core products, then it would be wrong to set a promotional objective of expanding sales of this particular brand, which is not part of the business's core product market. For instance, the Boots chain did this when it was seeking to concentrate on its pharmaceutical brands by pulling out of baby clothes products.

Time constrained

When planning any campaign, deadlines must be set for the achievement of the objectives. Deadlines help provide both the pressure to achieve the objectives, but also a means of assessing the success or failure of the campaign.

Areas of a business that use marketing objectives

The following is a list of general areas for which marketing objectives are often stated. Whilst the list is not comprehensive, it includes the main aspects of the business that marketing promotions are seeking to alter or improve.

- Profits
- Return on investment (%)
- Sales (in units) and turnover or revenue (£s)
- Market shares (%)
- Profit to sales ratios (%)
- Annual rates of growth of the above (%).

Ⓐ CTIVITY

Task

For each of the six areas above state a possible objective that will satisfy the SMART requirements for setting objectives. For instance, two per cent growth in profits over the next six months for sales of Mars bars would satisfy the requirements of being specific, measurable, achievable and time constrained. You cannot say it is relevant until you find out what the overall business aims are.

Promotional objectives

Whilst the objective areas covered above are acceptable objectives for a promotional campaign, there is a more focused aspect of promotional objectives which you need to be aware of. Often marketing and promotional objectives are used interchangeably; however, there may be times when the term 'promotional objectives' refers to a more specific set of criteria and these are covered below.

When designing promotional activities, it is important that you are aware of what the main promotional objectives are, as these will determine the ultimate content of the campaign and what is to be communicated. The main promotional objectives that businesses seek to achieve include the following.

Communicating information (inform, persuade, reinforce)

These three aspects of communication are often referred to as the three core objectives of any promotional campaign or activities. Consequently the planners must always bear in mind how the setting of other objectives relate to these three core aspects. So, for instance, if a business is seeking to increase customer loyalty in the face of competition, the ultimate communication method to be used is that of reinforcement, and this will in turn guide the content of the campaign methods and materials.

These are covered in greater detail in the promotions activities section of the book.

 Methods of communication, page 18

Changing attitudes and perceptions

Many promotions activities are geared towards achieving this objective. For instance, if sales have been dropping for a product and research has indicated that consumers see the product as being dated, the campaign must focus on correcting this and persuading them to purchase the product again. Marks & Spencer has had to make this a major objective for the past three years since they recognised sales were dropping, due in part to a change in consumer perception of their stores.

Creating and/or raising awareness of the business and/or its products

This objective is especially true for new product launches, but may also apply to existing businesses that have decided to diversify into new markets or geographical regions with existing products.

Promoting company image

With increased emphasis in recent years on social responsibility, many businesses have seen the need to promote corporate image in itself as a means of reinforcing loyalty and establishing a competitive edge over competitors.

CASE STUDY

Sustainability at Jaguar

A commitment to environmental and social responsibility is at the heart of the values that guide actions and activities across Jaguar. We believe we have taken a step forward in our understanding of what sustainable development means for the company. We also realise that there is still a long way to go before all the aspects of sustainable development become integrated into our day-to-day business activities.

13

By far the biggest challenge for Jaguar will be to continue to reduce the impact of our products. We are responding to this challenge with an investment in technical developments that will further reduce vehicle fuel consumption and emissions. Our aim is to be among the best within our premium market sector in terms of the environmental performance of the products that we offer our customers.

Jaguar's Sustainability Goal is to be amongst the leaders in demonstrating progress towards sustainability, by reducing the environmental burden, and contributing to a better quality of life for communities affected by the design, manufacture, use and disposal of Jaguar cars.

We are determined to continue to protect the environment and play a supporting role in our local communities with the same pride and passion that we utilise in the design, engineering and production of our cars.

Mike Beasley,
Managing Director

Need to do

You can look in more detail at Jaguar's policy aims and goals by logging on to their website at http://www.jaguarcars.com/uk/environment/html/index.html

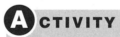 **A** **CTIVITY**

Task

Choose three other business organisations: using either the Internet or company reports, identify their goals relating to social responsibility and corporate image.

Promoting events

Especially in the service sector, but also in the launching of new products, promotion campaigns may involve the promotion of events rather than one product or brand. The success of such events will very much depend on careful planning. A good example of an event is the 'Match of the Day' Exhibition at the NEC in Birmingham, where the focus is on the BBC's main soccer programme but it involves many other products.

Attracting new customers

When a corporate objective may be expansion, and a marketing objective an increased market share, there may be a specific promotion objective of attracting new customers from a particular geographical area or for a particular brand. This shows how setting a hierarchy of inter-related objectives will enable planning to be more specific and hopefully successful.

In practice, such a hierarchy may not exist, and you will need to allow for the fact that many businesses will set promotion objectives which fit more into the marketing objective category.

Recruiting new employees

Sometimes a promotion campaign may not be directly connected with sales but with recruitment. This will obviously apply to the growing number of service sector businesses in the recruitment sector. However, some campaigns may involve the objective of recruitment as part of the campaign itself.

Need to know

Be careful to always examine the assessment criteria carefully to ensure that you are aware of the specific meaning of the terms used by the examination board you are being assessed by.

Setting out the objectives

The following case study illustrates the main objectives set for the launch of the new Kit Kat Chunky bar in 1999.

🅒ASE STUDY

Kit Kat Chunky launch

Objectives for the launch

A wise company will look to justify every new venture in strict business terms: it will set tough performance targets. These in turn can be converted into production targets, cost estimates and revenue projections. The purpose of this launch was to revitalise the Kit Kat Brand with a product which would not compete with existing Kit Kat products but with those of its competitors.

Quantitative objectives

Nestlé set demanding quantitative objectives for the launch. Nestlé aimed to:

- achieve 90% distribution in all sectors of the confectionery market within the first four weeks after the launch

- sell 50 million units (i.e. 2,750 tonnes of product) in 1999, the year of the launch
- increase sales in subsequent years.

Qualitative objectives

Nestlé also set several qualitative objectives. These were to:
- broaden the number of occasions on which people consume Kit Kat, with the vision that Kit Kat would be the natural choice for all breaks
- increase Kit Kat's market penetration by enticing new consumers to the brand, and by persuading lapsed users to return to the product, with particular emphasis on the 12–20-year-old segment
- create real innovation in the countline (snacks) market.

As previously mentioned, possibly the most important task for any planner, as with the formation of any plan in business, is to set SMART objectives for the campaign. Without SMART objectives, planning will lack direction and be less effective than should be the case. There are many objectives which could be set, and these are considered later in the book, but whatever they are, they must be clearly stated from the outset and managed so as to maximise both the benefits of any expenditure and sales revenue earned. Typical sales promotion objectives include:
- encouraging repeat purchase
- extending distribution
- combating competition
- persuading new customers to try out the product
- changing timings to smooth out peak buying periods.

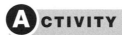

ACTIVITY

Task

Using the case study on the launch of the Kit Kat Chunky bar, assess the degree to which each of the objectives satisfy the SMART desirable features of setting objectives. Explain clearly the reasons for your comments.

 SMART, page 10

Need to know

The previous activity is a useful means of preparing yourself for planning your own promotional strategy. To gain the higher grades for your portfolio work you are required to critically evaluate your proposal, and by ensuring that all objectives set are SMART objectives you will provide a clear foundation on which to develop an effective strategy.

Timing

The timing of the promotional campaign is another vital aspect of the planning process. If the timing is wrong, the whole success of the campaign could be jeopardised. A good example of this is the campaign for Reebok using a prominent Irish footballer as the main focus. The campaign was timed to be launched just before the start of the 2002 World Cup to coincide with this footballer's involvement in the Republic of Ireland team. However, after a terrible row with the team's manager just before the start of the World Cup, the player was sent home. This action, coupled with the negative publicity, meant that the campaign had to be abandoned, resulting in the immediate loss of all the recording costs and contracts that had been purchased prior to his sacking as captain.

Need to do

- In your planning, clearly identify **when** the promotion activities should take place and **why** you believe these to be the best means of achieving the chosen objectives. (Help is given in the section on the selection of activities.)
- Include in your plan a contingency plan, which identifies what action should be taken in the event of an unexpected change, such as that described above.

Reviewing expenditure

Too often planning fails to determine costs, but concentrates instead on activities. Such an omission, or poor preparation, can make the whole planning process a waste of time and effort. Any spending should be analysed and clearly categorised according to the type of activity taking place. For instance, such questions include:

- how much revenue will be lost from existing customers through price reductions?
- how much will point of sale materials cost?
- what is the cost of new packaging brought in just for the campaign?

Without clearly measuring these costs it would be difficult to evaluate whether the campaign falls within a prescribed budget or, at the end of the campaign, how effective the campaign has been. This evaluation stage is vital to the sales promotion process and is covered in detail in a later section. The Reebok example highlights the need for a *contingency plan* to be formulated in the case of such sudden changes as those experienced. The delay in the launch of their campaign appears to indicate a lack of such a contingency plan being in place.

I Methods of communication and types of promotional activity

This is a huge area to cover and will form the basis for a great deal of your portfolio work. This area of the book will be broken down into specific areas for ease of study. However, as you would expect, many of the areas are inter-related, and therefore when studying one area you should consider the overlap into another. Many of the examination boards award higher marks for a portfolio that evaluates a number of marketing and promotional approaches. The areas covered here are:

- advertising
- public relations
- branding
- packaging
- sales and promotion
- direct marketing, and
- e-commerce.

Advertising

Promotion and advertising are terms that are often confused. It is important that you understand that advertising forms one of the many functions of promotion – advertising is **not** the same as promotion. However, advertising is probably the most common form of promotional activity and will be the one you will be most familiar with.

A CTIVITY

Task
Quickly write down five advertisements that stick in your mind. What is it about the adverts that make them memorable?

Advertisements are used to carry messages and normally will form part of a wider promotional campaign. What needs to be decided at the offset is which type of advertising is most suitable to reach or pass the message on to the potential consumer.

What is worth remembering is that we are all the focus of a vast amount of advertising. What is the best way to get a message about a product or service to you? Is it:

> **Key term**
>
> **Advertising** can be defined as any paid form of non-personal promotion transmitted through a mass medium. The sponsor should be clearly identified and the advertisement may relate to an organisation, a product or a service.
>
> Brassington and Pettitt

 Promotional campaign, page 3

- **television**
- **radio**
- **magazine, or a**
- **poster?**

What you need to decide upon now is the purpose of the advertisement. Is it to **persuade** or **inform**?

This will in part be dependent upon what the marketing objectives are (see previous section).

 Objectives, page 8

Need to do

- Find out what the organisation is hoping to achieve through its advertising campaign.
- Identify the different media that the organisation is using to communicate its messages.
- Identify the target audience that the organisation is intending to communicate with.

Creating an advertising campaign

All organisations will go through the process of deciding on an advertising campaign; it should include the following stages:

 Campaign, page 3

- Identify the target market for the organisation's goods or services.
- Define what the organisation hopes to achieve through the campaign.
- Decide what message the organisation wishes to communicate.
- Decide how much it is willing to spend.
- Carry out the campaign.
- Evaluate the effectiveness of the campaign.

This process is essential in choosing the most appropriate method or medium for an advertising campaign. Advertising is normally measured against the OTS (Opportunity To See). This relates to the amount of exposure an advertisement will get.

Consider the difference between the OTS of a poster placed in a local community centre and one shown at 7.30 p.m. on ITV. Obviously there would be a massive difference in exposure; however, what needs to be considered here is the intended outcome of the campaign.

CTIVITY

It is highly unlikely that Nike would advertise its latest trainers by putting posters on village notice boards. Why is this?

Choosing the right media

It is essential that an organisation communicates with customers effectively; to enable it to do this it needs to know certain information about the customers (age, sex, income, etc.), which will allow it to make some broad assumptions. These assumptions will include amongst others:

- the lifestyle a person leads
- how much they spend on certain goods
- the magazines they read
- the cars they drive.

All of this background information helps an organisation build up a picture of the type of advertising campaign they should embark upon. No organisation can afford to waste money on an advertising campaign; most will be looking to see what return on spending they will get. This may involve looking at the increase in sales or the number of visitors that has increased due to an advertising campaign. This issue will be dealt with in more detail when you consider evaluating promotional activity.

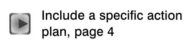 Include a specific action plan, page 4

CASE STUDY

Pizza Hut

Pizza Hut, the international fast food company, approaches promotion in two main ways. There is the national coverage approach, where television advertisements and posters are shown highlighting the latest pizza creation. This is carried out at HQ level. The second approach to promotional activities that Pizza Hut carry out is on a local level. Each store manager has a promotional budget with which they can decide on the most appropriate way of promoting the store locally.

This could include giving special offers or discounts to certain segments of the public; it could include deciding to advertise the store in a university magazine in an attempt to attract students. Whatever the method, there is a set rule that applies, which is that the promotion must generate at least two and half times the cost of the activity. For example, if a local Pizza Hut manager decided to spend £1,000 on advertising in the local university 'rag', it is expected that there will be an increase in sales directly related to that spent in the order of £2,500.

Ensuring the message is getting across depends on how it is being delivered. You will need to consider how well the organisation you are investigating is reaching its audience. You will also need to consider alternative methods of media and discuss why they may be more beneficial to the organisation or to a particular advertising campaign they are involved with.

Types of advertising media

Television allows a company to communicate with a broad and diverse range of potentially large audiences. This means that television has a relatively low cost per thousand (the cost of reaching a thousand viewers). However, due to its nature it shows no differentiation between the different groups that make up its audience.

> **Television**
> Television advertising presents a tremendous communication opportunity.
> Do you know of anyone who does not own a television?

A CTIVITY

Twenty thousand viewers may see a television advert. However, that is no indication that sales will rise by twenty thousand. Why is this?

It is also very difficult for organisations to monitor the audience's level of interest and understanding. There is no guarantee that the person watching the advertisement is following, learning or remembering it. Retention rates of information are therefore likely to be low so the advertisement needs to be repeated, which obviously increases the cost.

Advertisements also begin to compete with each other, to try and catch your attention during the brief moment between programmes. Almost every area of life is advertised, from hair to cars, so finding the right approach is essential if it is to engage the consumer. Organisations will research and develop advertising ideas and concepts to ensure they grab your attention.

The following case study looks at how a toilet-cleaning company goes about developing an advertising strategy.

C ASE STUDY

JEYES and the Bloo Loo advertising campaign

Creative advertising

Advertising toilet products is not easy. For most people, wash basins, WCs, kitchen sinks, U-bends, etc. lack the appeal of, say, pistes or pizzas. In the past, advertising for toilet products has tended to be functional and factual, but not much fun.

Since 1981, Bloo had been supported sporadically through a series of television campaigns that centred on the character of a 'talking loo'. Not all TV regions had carried these campaigns. Research showed that although consumers had only faint memories of the campaign (it had not been active for 5 years) many remembered the creative loo character. Jeyes felt that this could be the starting point for developing a new campaign.

Choosing the right media,
page 20

Genuinely creative TV advertisements can attract attention and have great impact. They also have the advantage of demonstrating to a huge audience the product actually in use. Better still, the growth of specialist cable and satellite channels has created specific audiences that can be targeted.

Faced with this promising prospect, a creative team developed the 'talking loo' character. He was given a camp and slightly 'affected' approach; Julian Clary supplied the voice-over. Most important, the character was developed in a way that encouraged humour and wit. Significantly, the team decided against 'toilet humour'. This decision enhanced the appeal of the advertising.

The camp male person of the toilet allowed the attributes of the products to be set out in a witty, cheeky, entertaining fashion. This approach was seen to connect with housewives in particular. More importantly, however, the advertising brought the Bloo brand up-to-date. The kind of language employed in the script had moved on from the 'Carry-On' tone of previous commercials to reflect a more modern version of camp humour.

Source: www.thetimes100.co.uk

Advertising campaigns normally play on the following factors:
- saving or making money
- fear avoidance
- humour
- sex
- self esteem/image.

Regulatory bodies,
page 47

There are obvious constraints regarding what can and cannot be included in advertising; this will be covered later when we address the issue of external constraints in promotion and marketing.

CASE STUDY

Carling Black Label – buy it or else!

The makers of Carling Black Label lager recently initiated a novel approach to persuasive advertising. The advertisement involved a number of famous personalities who were recognised as having a high annoyance value. The advertisement played on the fact that if you didn't purchase the lager then the personalities would be allowed to sing a song.

The advertisement worked exceptionally well in two ways:

Firstly, the humorous side of the advertisement made it memorable and helped consumers link the advertisement to the product.

Secondly, due to the nature and uniqueness of the advertising campaign it received a great deal of media publicity. The story of the advertisement was actually carried on the front page of two leading tabloid newspapers. This 'extra' promotion is what marketing departments dream of. The increased publicity was directly related to an increase in the sale of Carling Black Label lager.

Another of Carling's well-known advertisements is the 'Crab' advertisement.

'Cracking' opens in the aftermath of a plane crash on a desert island. The sole survivor, a man, is collapsed on the beach and we see him being roused by a friendly crab. To the man's amazement, the crab leads him to a fridge full of Carling, but his hopes are dashed when he discovers that the beer is warm. Undeterred, the man proceeds to build an incredible machine out of the debris lying around. The crab helps the man again by running round and round on the machine to create enough power for the fridge so that the survivor can quench his thirst with a long, cold refreshing pint of Carling.

Finally, the man settles down to watch the sun disappear over the horizon. He takes a long, lingering gulp of lager and ('crack'), tucks into a tasty meal of crab meat!

See http://www.bassbrewers.com/brands/carling.asp for more information.

Radio

Compared with television, radio normally offers a low cost per time slot alternative, but the effectiveness of the media is questionable. One of the main problems with radio is that there are many commercial stations; also, the advertising tends to be grouped so several advertisements will go out in one slot, making it difficult for the customer to take in specific information.

However, the cost of production can be low – it is normally broadcast to a local market (this is rapidly changing with the increase of national commercial radio), making it an accessible and attractive media for the small business advertiser.

Need to do

Contact your local commercial radio station and find out what the costs are to broadcast an advertisement. See how the rates change in relation to the time of broadcast and length of the advertisement.

Magazines

The major advantage of any printed material is that the information can be given and then revisited at the desire of the reader. How many times have you dug out old magazines and reread articles (even though the magazine may be a few months old)?

Further, how often do you borrow or lend your magazines to friends or colleagues?

Key marketing and
promotional terms,
page 70

The other major factor with magazine advertising is that it allows to a greater extent market segmentation. Magazines are produced with a customer in mind, whether they are plumbers or young males interested in football. This obviously makes printed promotion quite attractive, particularly when you consider the vast amount and range of magazines that there are available.

Magazines will normally fall into the following categories:

- general and news-based magazines – *The Economist*, *National Geographical*
- special interest magazines – *Bunty*, *Just Seventeen*, *Cosmopolitan*
- trade and technical journals – *Chemical Engineering*, *The Property Surveyor*.

Figure 2 © *The Economist Newspaper Limited, London, 8th September 2001; © National Magazine Company; Reprinted by special permission from Chemical Engineering, July 2002 cover*

Need to do

- Find out if your organisation subscribes to any particular magazines.
- Find out which printed publications they use to promote their products.
- Try and get a cost of advertising in a specific magazine that is relevant to the organisation you are investigating.

Internet and e-commerce

Very much a developing media and one that many organisations are embracing, advertising on the Internet is the fastest-growing promotional activity in marketing. If you consider the potential size of your audience it is easy to see why.

Internet advertising lifts many of the constraints that printed matter holds – it allows moving pictures as well as narrative information (see www.cocacola.co.uk and www.nike.com).

The major move has been to allow consumers to interact with the organisation, making the whole process of advertising and promotion an enjoyable and two-way process. However, the costs of developing and more importantly the up-keep of a site can be immense. On the positive side though, basic and cheap Internet advertising is available and can work very effectively for the smaller Internet advertiser.

Internet advertising and e-commerce (doing business electronically) is still in its development stage and does bring with it some problems. Hacking and security of data are two factors that major organisations have recently had problems with.

CASE STUDY

Egg customers boil over

Jill Insley on a furious revolt over the 'incompetent' internet bank's blunders

Egg, the internet bank, has attracted more than 1.8m customers in three years by offering low credit and high savings interest rates. But several readers who signed up are complaining of serious errors and bad service.

Customers say Egg has:

- 'lost' their money – in two cases thousands of pounds – in transit between accounts
- collected direct debits from the wrong accounts and returned payments incorrectly, resulting in unjustified but hefty interest charges for the account holders.

And, in all the cases reported, it has taken weeks, if not months, to respond satisfactorily. Many of those who have contacted us are now leaving Egg.

Jill Insley, *The Observer*, Sunday February 3, 2002
© *The Observer*

However, some organisations have readily welcomed the benefits that e-commerce as a promotional tool can bring, even to the extent of forsaking normal and well-established promotional routes such as television and magazines and adopting an 'E-only' approach to launching a product.

CASE STUDY

Kellogg's 'Real Fruit Winders'

This case study looks at the recent web launch of Kellogg's Real Fruit Winders. The launch had two main features. Firstly, it was done with key support from a website. Secondly, the product format is Kellogg's first move outside of cereals and cereal bars and into a totally new category of fruit snacks.

Real Fruit Winders are fun, fruit snack rolls. The primary target market for them is children aged 6–12. The Internet was chosen to communicate with the target audience because it is where children interested in games and technology are most likely to be found.

The campaign aimed to grab the attention of opinion formers and trendsetters who would then tell their peers. The campaign is particularly interesting because it was based around a set of animated characters that speak their own language. Also, these characters and their adventures were introduced to the target audience well in advance of the product they supported.

In a rapidly changing world, marketing specialists need to use state-of-the-art communication methods, particularly when dealing with young people who tend to be most familiar with the latest technology. The best way to launch a new product is to use the media most appropriate to the target audience. For example, magazines like *Bliss* and *Sugar* (targeted at teenage girls) are ideal vehicles for launching teenage cosmetics. Similarly, popular television programmes watched by a large proportion of the population provide suitable media for marketing mass-market consumer products like toothpaste and breakfast cereals.

Traditionally, firms have used television for product launches because it reaches into millions of homes. However, in an age in which the majority of homes have access to the Internet and where young people are the keenest online browsers, it makes sense to build a launch around digital media as well as television advertising with some products. Online games and competitions help remind consumers about a brand, but the difficult bit is how to persuade audiences to interact with these forms of branded entertainment in the first place; promotions such as animations, email campaigns and sponsorships need to be developed.

Source: www.thetimes100.co.uk

 Choosing the right media, page 20

ACTIVITY

Task

Carry out a SWOT analysis on Kellogg's approach to launching their new product.

Posters

Within this heading we will include advertising hoardings as well as transport-orientated media (advertising on buses and taxis). This form of advertising relies heavily on impact; it is often suggested that if a poster makes you stop and think then it has fulfilled its purpose!

It is often the case that poster campaigns will complement a wider advertising plan and reinforce the message. Its format is normally very visual (due to its nature) and its success can be measured by a person's 'dwell time' (how long people pause to look at it). Advertising posters can range from small DTP (desk top publishing) adverts to huge hoardings.

Hoardings are normally rented by the month, ideal locations being bus routes or busy commuter areas as this allows them to be seen many times by people passing. With the introduction of moving and video hoardings the possibilities for advertisers increase.

There are, however, certain potential drawbacks to hoarding as a medium for advertising.

> **Note!**
>
> Again, the factor to consider is which is the most appropriate method to meet your promotional objectives.

 Objectives, page 8

CASE STUDY

Wonderbra

The Wonderbra advertisement was a focus for much discussion following a number of accidents by motorists who were distracted by huge advertising hoardings showing a scantily clad model promoting the new Wonderbra. However, the publicity that this caused was not undesirable to Playtex, the makers of the Wonderbra, as it increased the awareness of the product. It did however receive a large number of complaints, which were forwarded to the Adverting Standards Authority.

> **Benchmark ASA cases**
>
> **Wonderbra (1994)**
> The Wonderbra campaign, featuring the model Eva Herzigova, prompted complaints that the adverts were offensive, but the ASA permitted them on the grounds they were clearly meant to be humorous.
> Source: www.guardian.co.uk

 ASA, page 47

Public relations

Public relations or PR is an immensely powerful tool that organisations ignore at their cost. In basic terms it fall into two distinct areas:

- Good PR – information that enhances the perception of a product/service or organisation, and
- Bad PR – information that damages the perception of an organisation, product or service.

Figure 3 on the next page illustrates a number of potential means that an organisation can employ to develop its PR image. The major benefit of this type of approach is that the organisation has some control over what material has been produced and what effect it may have on its consumers.

> **Key term**
>
> **Public relations** = the deliberate, planned and sustained effort to institute and maintain mutual understanding between an organisation and its public.
> *Source: The Institute of Public Relations*

Carling Black Label
case study, page 22

Need to know

Public relations can be formed through advertising; however this is not the best communication method for many types of people or for all objectives. The main method of PR is through a 'third party'. This may come in the form of a review, write up or investigation, for example. The main issue is that it is not directly controlled by the organisation.

Car manufacturers often dread the launch of a new model, particularly if they know that they are going to get a harsh review. Theatre producers dread the first night review of a new play. The main reason for this apprehension is that people will build a perception of the product or organisation based around these comments.

The public appreciates that organisations will put together sexy, glossy advertising campaigns to lure them. However, most consumers will hold a higher regard for an independent review. If you consider the power that such programmes as 'Watchdog' and 'Holidays from Hell' have, as well as magazines such as *Which,* in influencing consumer choice, you can begin to appreciate the importance of and the role of PR in an organisation's promotional plan.

Need to do

- See if you can find a press report or review of a product or service that your organisation has been involved with.
- What did the review say – how did it make you feel when thinking about the product or the organisation?
- Find out if the organisation sponsors any events and try and ascertain why they do this.

Magazines, page 23

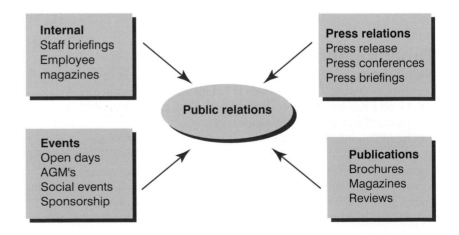

Figure 3 Techniques in public relations

Publicity itself may be unsought, such as when the tabloids get a hint of a scandal, whether it is huge pay rises or problems with products. This then leads to matters being publicised that perhaps the organisation would rather not have brought to light. To try and compensate for this, most organisations will attempt to develop good relationships with the media.

CASE STUDY

Regeneration agency under fire for 34% pay rise

Senior executives at a regional development agency (RDA) have been awarded pay rises of up to 34%, prompting calls by an MP for an investigation into the size of RDA pay packages.

There are nine RDAs – public bodies set up to stimulate economic regeneration in the English regions – and the pay rises, at Yorkshire Forward, triggered calls for an explanation by Helen Jackson, Labour MP for Sheffield Hillsborough.

Yorkshire Forward said Tom Riordan, director of strategy and policy, was awarded a package worth £89,925, while business development director, Susan Johnson, saw hers raised to £92,531, increases of 34% and 24% respectively.

The development agency initially said the rises were based on a performance-related scheme, but could not say what targets had been reached to justify the increases.

Later, it said Mr Riordan had been promoted to an executive director and that prompted his 34% increase, while Ms Johnson's pay rise was due to the board deciding to review her salary.

There was no explanation of how performance had been enhanced.

A spokesman said: "Whilst some directors receive large increases compared to those reported in previous accounts, this is a result of market level salaries based on an objective review being reflected for the first time in the accounts since Yorkshire Forward's creation in 1999".

The increases were in line with the civil service pay structures, he said, and reflected the employment market. All rises were government approved.

Ms Jackson said she wanted to know how the agency could justify handing out such large increases.

She is to ask the chief executive for an explanation of how Yorkshire Forward compares with other development agencies on salary package scales.

Paul Humphries, *The Guardian*, Friday August 23, 2002
© Paul Humphries

A CTIVITY

1 What damage do you feel that such pay rises may cause to the
   reputation of the company?
2 Do you feel the incident was reported fairly?

Need to do

- Obtain a copy of your local newspaper and identify any news
  stories which relate to local organisations. It may include stories
  about expansion, new products or profits.
- Decide for yourself if the coverage would be regarded as good or
  bad PR.
- What effect do you feel that this coverage may have on the
  organisation?

C ASE STUDY

Vodafone and Manchester United

The benefits of sponsorship

This case study examines how two businesses that have global
appeal are co-operating to achieve their shared visions for their
companies and brands. Vodafone hopes to become a global mobile
leader in terms of profit, customers and value, making mobile
networks the 'nervous system' of the networked economy spanning
three major developed markets (Europe, US and Japan). Manchester
United hopes to remain the most pioneering, best-supported and
most successful football club in the world.

   In the UK, Vodafone provides mobile telecommunications
products and services to three major groups of customers:

- private individuals
- small businesses
- large organisations.

Manchester United have been League Champions fifteen times and
European Champions twice, in 1968 and 1999. The club has won the
FA Cup a record ten times. It has six million fans in the UK and 50
million global fans.

   Vodafone's current business strategy is to grow through
geographical expansion, acquisition of new customers, retention of
existing customers and increasing usage through innovations in
technology. It is anticipated that by 2005 there will be over one billion

mobile phone users throughout the world, using a wide range of phones including 'third generation' and Wireless Application Protocol (WAP) enabled phones.

As a global telecommunications company Vodafone benefits from the advantages of operating across a range of markets, which enables them to benefit from huge cost savings as result of dealing with single suppliers worldwide, for example. Vodafone's marketing aim in the UK is to retain market leadership. Vodafone's strategy is product-led; the company is continually developing new products and services that utilise the latest technological advances.

However, as consumers become increasingly sophisticated users of modern mobile technology, they make new demands and seek added value through product improvements.

Both brands have a global appeal. Manchester United has a massive supporter base, including areas such as the Far East. These supporters represent potential customers for Vodafone. Clearly, the deal fits with Vodafone's marketing objectives of obtaining new customers, keeping its present ones and continuing to develop the brand.

Through the link with Manchester United, Vodafone has the opportunity to increase sales of phones and accessories. With a variety of 'Reds' phones and accessories, Vodafone is offering a range of Manchester United phone covers and cases with different designs. Thanks to manUmobile, fans have direct access through their mobile phone to the latest news from the club 24 hours a day.

Vodafone's sponsorship deal with Manchester United costs Vodafone £30 million over a four-year period. Vodafone clearly has to evaluate the effectiveness of this partnership in terms of its own marketing objectives.

Advantages of PR over advertising

Credibility

As previously mentioned, most consumers will appreciate that advertising is a method of persuasion in most cases, and that by using a certain shampoo you will not suddenly become devastatingly attractive to the opposite sex (or by driving a certain car your lifestyle will change to the one that is being advertised). The main reason is that advertisements are paid for by the organisation and it is reasonable to suggest that they will contain a certain bias. PR is seen as being free and, in the main, neutral.

Reach

If an organisation wished to embark on an advertising campaign that would have the same coverage as a mention on national television or

> **Note!**
>
> If a chemical company accidentally spilled chemicals into a local river, damaging the environment, it would without doubt receive coverage. If, however, they have prepared the details of what an excellent track record on safety they have as well as using the media attention to mention how they will rectify and improve the situation, then the focus is turned from the incident and placed upon how the organisation is reacting.

The recent Anthrax scares around the world had a beneficial knock on effect for a small UK firm specialising in portable, inflatable decontamination tents. The company received national and international coverage. This amount of exposure would have been far beyond the reach of such an organisation. It resulted in an unprecedented amount of demand for the products, leading to full order books for over two years and expansion of the organisation.

 Contingency plan, pages 3, 17

 How to evaluate a promotional activity, page 54

 Budgets, page 42

Budget
Attitude
Media coverage
Sales
Share price
Response generation

Figure 4 Measures of PR success

radio it would involve a multimedia strategy that would be extremely costly. A good PR initiative, which captures the interest of the media, will receive a massive level of reach. Even a relatively small firm can benefit from this.

Disadvantages of PR over advertising

Uncontrollability
Advertising allows complete control over what is said, how it is said and where it is said; the control of publicity is in the hands of the media. A company or organisation can offer material to the media, but there is no guarantee that the media will take it on board, or how they will represent it.

Most large organisations make a contingency plan, which normally operates as a damage limitation exercise. Senior managers will be briefed on how to deal with the media or how to conduct themselves at press briefings. In some cases careful preparation of such exercises can have its benefits. The real skill is to turn a negative into a positive.

Evaluating the success or failure of PR
As with any promotional activity, an organisation needs to be able to evaluate the process at the end, to ascertain if objectives have been met or not. Haywood (1984) suggested some commonly used measures of success.
- Budget – has the PR activity been completed within the given budget?
- Attitude – through research the perception of the organisation or product can be measured to see if it has improved.
- Media coverage – establishing how much media coverage has been achieved (measured by airtime or columns/pages in a newspaper or magazine). It is also important to evaluate the type of coverage – what is it? Is it favourable/complimentary or did it criticise?
- Sales – this is probably the most important measure of an organisation's success, and the effect of PR on sales can be evaluated.
- Share price – how have the value or demand for shares altered during the PR exercise?
- Response generation – how many enquires into the product or service have been generated?

Branding

Need to do

Can you identify a logo or symbol that the organisation you are investigating uses to identify itself or its products?

Creating and developing a brand is a huge business at the moment. The theory behind developing a brand is that it makes it easier to buy or sell your products. Organisations will attempt to develop brand loyalty as this in turn creates repeat custom.

Popular brands are often supported by what are known as 'strap lines' or 'catch lines'. Can you identify the following?

- Just do it
- Because you're worth it
- They're grrreat!
- The drive of your life.

There are three main types of branding that organisations use.

Multiple product branding

This is where only one brand name is used for a range of products. This allows a range of products to be built under one brand and further allows the strength and perception of one product to be transferred to other products. It also allows new products to be more easily launched. Organisations such as Sony, Dyson, Levi's and Cadbury's use this method.

Retailers own brand

This is where the organisation retailing the product will put its name to the product. Own brands have seen huge changes, particularly in the food market. The original concept was that own brands offered a cheaper alternative to the well-known 'super brands'. In the mid-nineties many supermarkets developed their own value brands which consisted of plain packaging and a 'no frills' approach. Their main selling point was price; as with any competitive market all supermarkets had their own value brands.

In more recent times, retailers own brands have focused on the opposite end of the market, developing what have become known as 'finest' ranges. These are products that command a premium price and compete directly with the quality super brands.

Multiple branding

This involves a firm using a range of brand names for its products. Nestlé, Mother's Pride and Mars all have a number of brands. This allows them to develop brands for particular markets. Its main advantage is that if one particular brand should fail then the effect should not be felt on the other brands.

Detergents and washing powders are an excellent example of multiple branding, the majority of high street-named washing powders are owned and produced by two manufacturers. This in some cases leads to brands competing against each other, however if the end result is an increase in sales then the objective has been met.

They're grrreat! is a registered trademark of Kellogg Company
for breakfast cereals and is reproduced by permission of Kellogg Company.

Figure 5 Kenwood is a registered trademark of Kenwood Marks Limited; The Orange device is a registered trademark of Orange Personal Communications Services Limited.

Key term

A brand is any name, style, words or symbols, singly or in any combination that distinguish one product from another in the yes of the consumer.
Brassington and Pettitt

Need to know

Brand recognition is an important factor of the promotion of any organisation. It allows that organisation to differentiate itself from competitors. It should also represent what the organisation is about and make it instantly recognisable. This should build up trust, and make the product more consumer friendly.

Need to do

Develop a strap line and symbol that you feel represents the type of organisation or product you are investigating.

Developing and maintaining a brand are of crucial importance to organisations, as the CORUS case study highlights.

CASE STUDY

CORUS

The importance of building a strong brand image

A brand usually carries a logo or trademark by which it is recognised. Developing a corporate brand is important because a positive brand image will give consumers and other interested stakeholders confidence about the full range of products and activities associated with a particular company.

Advertising can help create or reshape an image, but personal experience and the comments of other users represent the reality behind the image and, as such, are even more powerful.

Corus was created through the merger of the UK's British Steel, and Dutch company Hoogovens, in October 1999. The merger created an innovative metals company that combined international expertise with local knowledge.

Choosing the new name was a long, careful consultative process. The first step was to identify the values of both companies and to encapsulate them in the name and logo.

The consultation established:

- the views of customers, suppliers and employees
- those aspects of the existing organisation of which they were most proud.

While the name and logo would clearly be the most visible aspects of the new organisation, they would need to be supported by key features of the organisation e.g. behaviour, attitude, ways of working, to meet the needs of customers. Branding works because customers' choices are based on emotion as well as logic.

The new mark is used in Corus's advertising, marketing, promotions, brochures, on uniforms, vehicles, signs, stationery and is even stamped onto products. The intention is to etch the mark into customers' consciousness.

(A)CTIVITY

1 Why do you think Corus place such a huge emphasis on developing a logo and brand identification?
2 What benefits to Corus can you see in the organisation having a recognisable logo?

Packaging

Packaging is a vital part of the product and the promotional strategy of an organisation. It not only serves a functional role of protecting the product but also serves as a means of communicating information and brand to the consumer and therefore has a promotional function. Packaging is often the first contact with consumers; it is therefore essential that it is appropriate and attractive.

Consider the row upon row of chocolates, biscuits, washing powder, magazines or toilet rolls in an average supermarket. Producers want their product to stand out and to catch the consumer's eye. In this environment packaging can make or break the success of a product. If the packaging doesn't work – either by not containing the goods adequately or not being attractive enough, then the consumer is likely to reject the product. Successful packaging can be achieved through creative use of materials, text and colour.

Packaging also acts as a powerful communication device; it can be used for promoting competitions, other products, samples and gifts. A popular move has been the 'instant win' promotions from the producers of confectionary and drink manufacturers. In this approach the packaging itself contains a prize, whether it be contained in the wrapper (as with Mars bars) or under the ring pull (as with Coke and Grolsch).

As mentioned at the outset these promotional methods of communication do not operate in isolation. Packaging, regardless of the product, should combine some form of branding, whether it be food or steel.

The following case study looks at the importance and role that packaging has in a competitive and consumer-led market.

Figure 6 ® MARS is a registered trademark © Masterfoods

Figure 7 © Kellogg Company

Choosing the right media, page 20

CASE STUDY

Heinz Foods

Consumers' buying habits reflect their personality, income, age, lifestyle and aspirations. Heinz has a series of icon products that are brand leaders and with which the company is closely associated, e.g. salad cream, baked beans, tomato ketchup.

This case study shows how the popularity of Heinz' core icon products has been maintained and enhanced, by developing aspects of the product or brand to keep them relevant and satisfying for modern consumers.

By bottling horseradish in clear glass jars Henry Heinz was clearly different to other manufacturers who bottled their goods in coloured glass jars to hide the cheap fillers used to add to the ingredients. This was the first move to meeting consumers' needs and underpinning Heinz values of offering quality products.

When managing a large range of products serving several markets, firms must develop ways of analysing the performance of these products. Changes in consumer tastes mean that even though products such as Heinz Tomato Ketchup have staying power, there is always a demand for new products. Refreshing existing concepts through innovation extends the way in which products are used and consumed.

Firms need to use their knowledge of their market to:
- identify gaps and trends in existing and new markets
- develop creative ideas.

The key functions of any pack are to provide the consumer with a functional concept that protect its contents in transit, storage and use. Heinz Microwaveable Pasta Meals are aimed particularly at busy working women who are 'on the go' and looking for a satisfying, quick meal that is convenient and healthy. Over 90% of people have access to a microwave at work, and the number of households owning microwaves has increased by 50% in the last ten years.

Not surprisingly, product development is concentrating on convenience and speed without loss of taste or quality. The soups can be heated in two minutes – and eaten directly and conveniently from the microwaveable bowl.

Key term

Sales promotion refers to '... a range of tactical marketing techniques designed within a strategic marketing framework to add value to a product or service in order to achieve specific sales and marketing objectives'.
Institute of Sales and Promotion

Sales promotion

Sales promotions are the incentives offered to consumers to encourage them to buy goods or services. Due to their nature they are normally short term, to give a boost to sales or help launch a new product or break into a new market. Most consumers are on the lookout for a 'bargain'. The attractiveness of sales promotions gives the consumer the feeling they are achieving this. There are a variety of sales promotions that an organisation could use.

Once again, the deciding factor in selecting one or more of the following should be its suitability for the organisation, goods or service you are investigating:

Competitions – the entry to many competitions is through the purchase of the product; for example, an entry form may be printed on the back of a pack of cereal. Newspapers also use this method regularly, offering huge prizes of cash or property to readers of their publication.

Free offers – again aimed at our 'consumer bargain instinct', the feeling that we are getting something for nothing is normally irresistible. Buy one get one free (BOGOF) is an increasingly popular method of promotion.

Coupons or refunds – this approach has seen the link-up of many organisations in very different markets; for example, the purchasing of a breakfast cereal may allow you cheap entry into a theme park. Some coupons will give money off a repeat purchase, almost tying the consumer into buying the product again.

Product placement – companies will pay to have their products placed strategically on film sets and TV programmes. The recent movie Men In Black 2 featured the product placement of Rockport and Ray Ban sunglasses throughout the movie. This link with the movie and the product is most valued by organisations as it normally leads to increased sales if the film is a success.

Special credit terms – the 'buy now pay later' schemes are exceptionally popular as they move the physical outlay of payment. They offer a huge incentive to potential consumers and can influence greatly the choice of organisation they make their purchase from.

Mission statement page 9

Need to know

Sales promotion is a short-term method of increasing sales or awareness of a good or service; it can allow organisations to break into new markets, or extend the product lifecycle of an existing product.

Need to do

Identify any sales promotion activities that the organisations you are investigating have undertaken and attempt to evaluate how successful they were.

ACTIVITY

Can you think of any sales promotion techniques that would benefit the organisation?
Ask yourself why you feel they would be suitable.

Direct marketing/selling

Direct marketing has seen a dramatic increase in popularity by many
leading organisations – until the advent of e-advertising direct marketing
was the fastest growing promotional activity.

Direct marketing occurs when sales are made directly with the
organisation, i.e. there are no middlemen. This enables consumers to
make purchases from their own homes. Due to the fact that many
leading organisations have adopted the direct marketing as well as more
traditional methods, the choice for consumers has increased
dramatically.

The increased use of credit cards by consumers for purchasing, and
the need to be able to shop at what might be regarded as unusual hours,
have all helped to increase the demand for direct marketing. The
obvious benefit to the organisation is cost, as there are no intermediaries
in the supply chain. The producer is able to control its own marketing
and also has a chance to reach consumers who might not otherwise have
bought from the shop.

Direct marketing is also advantageous for specialist or niche markets
where specific consumers can be communicated to, without the need for
large and costly advertising to non-relevant consumers.

Methods of direct marketing

Telesales

This involves ringing people up at home or work and attempting to sell
them goods or services. This is an extremely cheap form of marketing
and allows the consumer to deal personally with the organisation. It can,
however, be regarded as intrusive. Telesales is often used for double
glazing and financial services.

Personal selling

This is where a representative of an organisation will attempt to promote
and sell products or services through personal contacts. The perceived
view is of a door-to-door sales person, however, this is only part of the
picture.

CASE STUDY

Alstom

Alstom produces gas turbines for the industrial markets around the
world. Most of the orders they deal with are multi-million-pound
transactions; the turbines themselves are exceptionally complex and
intricate. Alstom require sales representatives to be skilled engineers
to ensure they can answer or deal with any issues or queries that a

potential customer might have. It also allows customers to be dealt with as individuals. Each gas turbine will be required to work in varying locations and to do a variety of jobs; this individual approach ensures that the consumer is getting exactly what they want.

However, the costs of this type of direct selling can be expensive, face-to-face meetings all over the world incur a great deal of hotel and flight costs, it is only because the product itself carries such a high value that Alstom can afford to operate in this manner.

Catalogues

A well-established and proven means of marketing, catalogues have seen resurgence of favour recently. This is in part due to designer brands now being available from catalogues as well as the likes of the *Next Directory* offering quality clothing through mail order. Catalogues are also very popular with smaller producers, as they allow a full range of their brands with pictures and narrative to be sent directly to a targeted market. The improvement of the infrastructure behind catalogues, such as next day delivery and on-line ordering, make it a favourable method for a range of organisations.

Direct response advertisements

This method of marketing is based on consumers being encouraged to place orders after seeing advertisements in newspapers, magazines and on the television and radio. Mobile phone sales have seen a huge increase through this type of selling, the advertisement must carry enough information to encourage people to contact them.

QVC, the digital shopping channel is a ground-breaking direct response advertiser. Goods are shown, used and described and consumers can call and order directly. The advantage of shopping from home and the ease of purchasing all add to the experience for the consumer.

Direct mail

This involves the posting of promotional material to people's homes and work places. The material will relate to a specific product or service. The goods or service can then be acquired and are sent direct to the customer. Organisations use mailing lists which are normally cold contacts, that is, where no previous contact has been made by the organisation or derived from some previous research.

Direct mail has the following benefits:
- Personalised communication.
- Targeted markets or consumers.
- Detailed information can be provided.

It also has a number of disadvantages:
- The amount of direct mail has increased massively over recent years and can be of annoyance to some consumers.
- The mailing list can be out of date.
- It can regarded as a waste of paper.

Organisations, particularly charities such as Great Ormond Street and Oxfam, have benefited greatly from direct mail and have been able to raise large sums from people who have made donations. The problem arises when a household is asked by ten or twenty deserving charities a year to make a donation.

Promotional communication round-up

As has been mentioned throughout this section of the book, it is essential that organisations use the right type of communication. If they fail to they will:
- miss out on potential customers
- fail to maximise their promotional potential
- incur costs that will not yield rewards.

Factors to consider

Objectives, page 8

- Consider the promotional objectives you or the organisation has set.
- Consider the budget that has been allowed for promotion.
- Consider the type of consumer you are attempting to attract.
- Consider the brand and how it will be best represented.

One of the most well-known organisations in the world that use direct selling and promotion is Amway.

CASE STUDY

Amway

Amway has helped millions of people around the world to start their own independent businesses, through which they engage in person-to-person marketing. Amway makes good use of the technique.

Amway is different from the more traditional distribution channels in that the business has developed through direct selling. Amway has over three million Independent Business Owners (IBOs) worldwide. IBOs deal directly with clients, build up personal relationships and deliver direct to clients' homes. IBOs are highly motivated, selling to people they know or meet. The personal contact and care that they provide is an important element in direct selling. IBOs are self-employed and can introduce others to the business, and so form their own sales network.

I Influences upon promotional activities

The success or failure of any promotional campaign will, in part, be determined by the influences upon it from within and without the organisation. This is called the marketing environment and these influences must carefully be considered and taken into account at the planning stage or the campaign may seriously miss out on achieving its objectives.

The main influences that must be considered can be split into two main types: internal and external. Internal influences are those variables that the business has a control over and so can be reasonably easy to assess and implement into the planning process. External influences are ones that are beyond the control of the organisation and must be carefully observed and interpreted to ensure that the promotion campaign is as relevant and successful as possible.

The main internal influences

The corporate aims of the organisation
These are usually found in the mission statement of an organisation and state the ultimate aim for the business. Corporate aims are the responsibility of the senior executive decision-makers of an organisation and all objectives set at both strategic and tactical level emanate from these corporate aims.

 Mission statement, page 9

The main objectives of the promotional activity
These are the targets that a business will hope to achieve with regard to three main groups of objectives: informing, persuading and reinforcing actions, which lead to the consumer either purchasing the product in question, repeat buying or adopting the ideas being communicated.

 Communicating information, page 13

The results of market research
Any promotional activity should always follow from the results of market research. Market research is the process of asking and answering questions relating to the product or market that the organisation is involved in. The more accurate and up to date the information, the more likely it is that the marketing team will have an awareness of what the customers want and how best to meet their needs.

 Sections in a promotional plan, page 5

What message is to be communicated in the promotional activity
When putting a promotional campaign together the team must ensure that objectives are linked to the target audience and be aware of what stage they have reached in the stages of the purchase cycle. If research

has indicated that potential customers lack information about the product, then the message being communicated must concentrate on informing customers. Without an understanding of what the message should be, the campaign is likely to falter.

A clear identification of the target market

Market research, both primary and secondary, should help determine whom the target audience is for the product/products being promoted. This may consist of several groups of customers, not just one definable group. Consequently there may be a need for more than one message to be communicated in more than one way for the campaign to be fully effective. This is essential to ensure that the level of the message is right and the correct media is chosen to deliver the message.

The size of the promotional budget

Expense budget, page 4

This is often a major constraint on any marketing activity, and in your investigations you will need to glean information relating to the method of budget setting and the existence of any budget constraint within the business. Some businesses set aside a stated budget for marketing, and this is not negotiable. This will obviously determine what is or is not possible in terms of the size of any promotional campaign or activity.

Other businesses base their budget upon the perceived need, and so research what is required to achieve its stated objectives and then allocate a budget to ensure the objectives are achieved.

CASE STUDY

M&S ready for £20m of profile boosting

Marks & Spencer plans a £20 million advertising campaign to win back disaffected customers, and may sell up to 40 of its stores in an effort to raise £250 million.

The moves emerged at the weekend as new chief executive Peter Salisbury continues his bold strategy to restore profits and reputation at the ailing retail empire. Last month, Mr Salisbury wielded the axe over 31 of the group's most senior executives, including three directors, and said he was exploring whether M&S should offer designer clothing to regain lost sales.

Creating an advertising campaign, page 19

The advertising campaign – nearly double the normal M&S promotional budget – will use TV, radio and newspapers, and focus on products. Traditionally M&S has focused on local promotions for new stores. In the past 12 months it spent £12 million on advertising, £5 million of that promoting new outlets.

The group has not previously used national TV advertising, apart from a short campaign last Christmas to promote its January sale.

The advertising push is the brainchild of marketing director James Benfield, who was promoted to the role by Mr Salisbury. A spokeswoman for M&S said it had not yet been decided whether to use celebrity endorsements.

M&S has had a low-key approach to advertising and even shunned attention-grabbing window displays, preferring to rely on the pulling power of its brand and reputation for value.

The company is also considering selling 40 of its smaller stores, such as those in Bath and Oxford. It will not vacate the premises but lease them back, hoping to raise up to £250 million.

Julia Finch, *The Guardian*, Monday March 22, 1999

© *The Guardian*

ACTIVITY

The planned advertising campaign was almost double the normal promotion budget for M&S.

1 To what extent were the troubles being faced by M&S a result of their low promotion budget?

2 Using the article and your understanding of promotion and budgets, explain whether the doubling of the budget will guarantee success for M&S in their campaign to win back disaffected customers. If not, qualify your answer with reasons why success may not be guaranteed.

The timescale for the promotional activity

The timescale set for the promotional activity, and equally importantly, the achievement of the objectives, will be a major influence upon the promotional campaign. If competition is intense and the business has limited time in which to prepare and run the campaign, this could have a large bearing upon how successful the campaign is.

 Time constraints, page 12

The main external influences

Social influences

The marketing environment is greatly affected by social change and these must be carefully considered when putting a promotional plan together. It is normal to break the social influences into two key areas: demographic influences and cultural influences:

Demographic factors

Demographic factors relate to population size and make-up. Whilst the pace of change of these two aspects tends to be gradual over time, they

 Choosing the right media, page 20

have powerful impacts on both the volume of demand and the nature of demand and so should be carefully studied. Marketers have to be aware of the main demographic factors affecting most markets, especially in the western developed world. The key common factors are:

- population age distribution
- geographical shifts (especially related to deindustrialisation) and
- household composition.

Cultural factors

The make-up of a society's beliefs, values, attitudes and perceptions will vary from country to country and even regionally within a country. Marketers must be aware of the cultural norms of each society they are involved with and use this understanding as a basis for preparing relevant marketing materials. Whilst cultural change tends to be slow in terms of the key features, there is often room for persuasion to be used to change secondary values and beliefs.

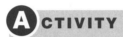

ACTIVITY

Consider the various social influences mentioned above and write a paragraph explaining why it is important to consider the social influences. What impact would it have on the success of the promotion activities if they were ignored?

Economic factors

The economic environment is prone to great change over time, triggered by a variety of events, and is one of the most difficult areas to account for when putting together a promotion campaign. If the product you are selling is deemed to be a luxury good, a recession in the economy will certainly mean there is a strong likelihood that your product's sales will fall. Marketers should take note of this relationship when planning any marketing campaign.

Figure 8 opposite, taken from the UK Government sustainable development website, shows the index of national output figures for the UK from 1970 to 2001 and would be a useful starting point for helping predict likely changes in the rate of growth of the economy.

Interest rates are also very important to consider when planning promotional activities. Interest rates are both the cost of borrowing and the reward for saving. If interest rates are low, then it is likely that people will tend to save less and spend more. Reinforcing this will be the fact that low interest rates also make borrowing cheaper, and so spending on goods and services will increase, especially the purchase of goods bought on credit. A chart of changes in the Bank of England's base rate from March 1998 to August 2002 is shown opposite in Figure 9.

Changes in exchange rates must also be carefully monitored, especially where products and materials are imported or exported. A sudden rise in

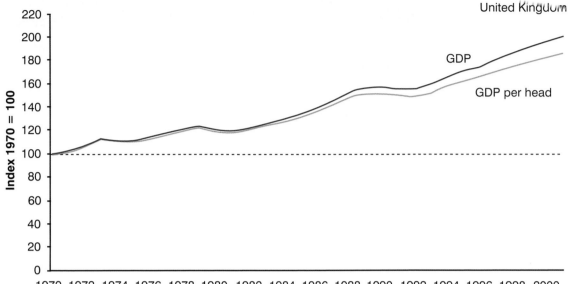

Source: Office for National Statistics   Based on constant 1995 prices
http://www.sustainable-development.gov.uk/indicators/headline/h1.htm

Figure 8 GDP and GDP per head: 1970–2001

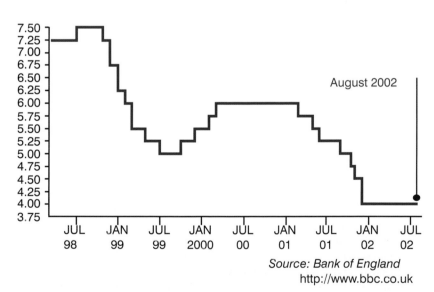

Source: Bank of England
http://www.bbc.co.uk   *Figure 9* Bank of England's base rate

the value of the pound sterling against the euro will make exports from the United Kingdom more expensive and could result in a fall in the demand for goods and services shipped for sale to Europe.

Need to do

- Find out what a) the current base interest rate and b) the exchange rate of pound sterling against the euro and the dollar are today.
- Prepare a figure and chart of how these have changed over the past year. These changes may be useful to help explain why promotional campaigns you are evaluating may not have been as successful as was originally anticipated.

Legislative factors and regulatory bodies

These two influences are combined here because of the way in which they overlap. If there was no legislation there would not be any great need for a regulatory body to monitor and adjudicate on whether a promotions communication is legal or not. There are over 150 different pieces of legislation relating to promotional practices, therefore any promotional campaign must bear these in mind before the messages are communicated.

The Office of Fair Trading (OFT) is specifically responsible for investigating breaches of legislation and, if necessary, prosecuting offending businesses. Usually, however, such businesses will be warned by industry-associated regulatory bodies such as the Advertising Standards Authority (ASA) and the Independent Television Commission (ITC) before the need for the OFT to act. These are considered later in the book in the section on promotional activities.

CASE STUDY

Court backs ASA in Ribena Tooth Kind case

The makers of Ribena Tooth Kind will no longer be able to claim that the product does not cause tooth decay, the high court ruled today.

In a landmark case, the drinks company lost its battle to overturn an Advertising Standards Authority ruling, published in July 2000, that its claim was misleading. The ASA had asked the advertisers to delete the claim made in a trade press advertisement that "Ribena Tooth Kind does not encourage tooth decay". The ASA also asked the advertisers not to repeat a poster advertisement showing Ribena Tooth Kind bottles as bristles on a toothbrush, because, without a qualifying statement, it implied that the product actively benefited oral health.

Drugs giant SmithKline Beecham, which owns Ribena, took the ASA's ruling to a judicial review because it believed it should be allowed to carry on making the claims. The company said it had the support of the British Dental Association, which had accredited the product.

But Mr Justice Hunt today said the claim "cannot be justified in such terms", adding, "the ASA were not only justified in coming to their conclusion but were duty bound to do so".

The ruling will delight parents and consumer watchdogs who have campaigned for clear and honest labelling on products, particularly those targeting children.

"I am delighted that the court has upheld our adjudication. The ASA has been vindicated and this judgement acknowledges that we conduct ourselves in a thorough and professional manner," said Christopher Graham, director general of the ASA.

"The outcome is a boost for the self-regulation of non-broadcast advertising and should increase confidence in the ASA's independence and ability to deliver sound and well thought through adjudications," he added.

The Hon Mr Justice Hunt said in his judgement: "This was indeed an absolute claim and is acknowledged to be so. It cannot be justified in such terms and the ASA were not only justified in coming to their conclusion but were duty bound to do so." The judge rejected a claim that an expert adviser employed by the ASA was biased against SmithKline Beecham and that the ASA had not given proper weight to the British Dental Association, which had accredited the product.

Claire Cozens, *The Guardian*
Wednesday January 17, 2001
© *The Guardian*

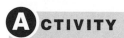

Tasks

1   What were the main problems with the original Ribena advertising?
2   What role did the ASA play in the Ribena case?
3   Would a Government regulatory body rather than a private body such as the ASA be better for monitoring and regulating advertising practices? Explain your views clearly, identifying advantages and disadvantages.

Regulatory bodies (including ASA, ITC and OFT)

Legislation, ASA and complaints

Regulatory bodies are not only involved with monitoring what is legal; they also look at ethical issues and advise or adjudicate on promotions which, though not breaking a law, cause sufficient offence that they are deemed unethical.

When evaluating sales promotion activities, whether your own or
those of another organisation, you need to differentiate between legal
and ethical aspects and clearly evaluate the communications materials
for both issues.

The following case study reveals the extent of the role that the ASA
plays in regulating advertising.

 ASE STUDY

FCUK leads the way as advert complaints soar

The number of advertisements to provoke the ire of consumers rose
sharply last year, as regulators dealt with the impact of new media
such as the internet and mobile phones.

Complaints relating to almost 10,000 advertisements reached the
advertising standards authority last year, which upheld its first
complaint against a mobile phone text message alert.

The ASA, which used its annual report to publish a list of the 40
most significant advertisements to influence its work over the past 40
years, revealed that complaints about junk mail overtook posters as
the medium to attract the most complaints.

A direct mail advert for slimming pills produced by Health
Laboratories of North America attracted the most complaints, with 211
irate customers calling the ASA. The most high profile controversy
surrounded French Connection, whose fcuk campaign continued to
cause controversy and resulted in 142 complaints. In both cases, the
advertisers were censured by the ASA.

But Lord Borrie, chairman of the ASA, warned against reading too
much into the number of complaints about any given advert. "These are
just a handful of the total volume of cases handled by the authority and
very few advertisements attract such large numbers of complaints."

In the past year advertisements for leisure-related products and
services accounted for the most complaints, with an increase from the
previous year of 37% to 2,904. Computer and telecommunications
products moved up from third to second place with 1,732 complaints,
while health and beauty products slipped to third, attracting 1,199
complaints.

Some 651 adverts were found to be in breach of the rules, 6.5% of
all the complaints that were resolved. This was a fall from 755 (8.8%)
in 2000.

The French Connection campaign continued to cause controversy: the fashion retailer now has its advertisements pre-vetted. "The ASA has consistently ruled against the use of fcuk as an expletive or a substitute word in a sentence," the authority said in its annual report.

Technological advances mean the ASA is now regulating ads that appear on the Internet, such as banners, pop-ups and commercial emails. In November it censured an SMS text advert for the first time, from the computer game firm Eidos. The message stated: "Please report to your local army recruitment centre immediately for your 2nd tour of duty. Commandos 2 on PC, It's More Real Than Real Life – out today." The complainant, a former soldier, said the message could cause undue fear and distress.

The report is the ASA's 40th and it highlighted adverts such as a claim by the makers of Maltesers, who claimed in 1959 about their product: "The chocolates with the less fattening centres!" Such claims must be backed up by documentary evidence, the ASA said.

Matt Wells, *The Guardian*, Thursday May 2, 2002
© *The Guardian*

Benchmark ASA cases

Ribena Toothkind (1998)
SmithKline Beecham took the ASA to the high court after it upheld complaints against adverts claiming the drink was nearly as kind to teeth as water. The court backed the ASA.

Marlboro (1975)
The cowboy was the brand's defining image, but he no longer features in UK tobacco adverts which are banned from glamorising the habit.
Source: www.guardian.co.uk

Ⓐ CTIVITY

For a more in-depth look at the effects of legislation on promotional activities you may wish to look at the article in the Appendix 'Pharmacia & Upjohn'.

Need to do

An in-depth summary of legislation relating to promotions activity can be found by accessing the following websites:
www.adassoc.org.uk or www.communicationsbill.gov.uk

Pressure groups

Pressure groups have become increasingly vociferous in recent years and any promotional materials should take into account likely pressure group opposition before being communicated. The Internet has made it possible for pressure groups to inform the public instantly of any issues relating to their concerns and this has meant that businesses have to consider likely opposition to their practices very carefully.

The following case study highlights the work of the pressure group 'Labour behind the Label' against clothing manufacturers exploiting cheap Far East labour.

 Public relations, page 27

ASE STUDY

Help workers stitched up by the big brands

Campaigners for improved wages and conditions for clothing workers in developing countries are capitalising on the Euro 2000 football tournament to build awareness of these oppressed workers' plight. Postcards addressed to England manager Kevin Keegan, the England team, David Davies of the Football Association and Chris Ronnie, the chief exec of sportswear brand Umbro, are being circulated by a pressure group called Labour behind the Label.

Labour behind the Label is the UK platform of the pan-European Clean Clothes Campaign, which aims to draw attention to oppressive wages and conditions that workers face in sportswear factories in the far east and central America. Workers in these sweatshops earn just £2.80 a day to stitch the shirts that sell for £45 in the UK. It would cost just 16 million euro (£9.7m) to double the salary – for a 40 hour week – of 50,000 workers in the garment industry in Indonesia. That is half of the sponsorship money negotiated with the Dutch national team in 1999 and less than 2% of Nike's entire advertising and promotion budget for 1999.

Nick Pandya, *The Guardian*, Saturday June 17, 2000
© *The Guardian*

CTIVITY

1 What are the main areas that Labour behind the Label is opposed to?
2 How might this opposition affect the sale of Nike and Umbro clothes?
3 How effective, in reality, do you think this pressure group is likely to be, given the importance of designer clothes for consumers? Explain your answer.

Need to do

If you wish to investigate the work of pressure groups opposed to clothing manufacturers further, you could look at material on the following website: http://www.cleanclothes.org.

Competitors

The likely actions of competitors should always be considered with any promotional activity you are proposing or implementing. It is highly unlikely that any competitor will sit back and not respond to a promotion campaign that is likely to threaten its market position and share. This is clearly shown in the highly competitive financial services industry. If one bank lowers its interest rates it is usually not long before other banks offer similar or even better discounts and rates.

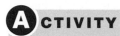

CTIVITY

Investigate the way in which supermarket chains Sainsbury, Tesco, Morrisons and Asda have competed over the past five years. In particular, identify new promotional activities and how the others have responded.

Technological factors

The development of technologies such as digital electronics (including computer-aided manufacturing and design) has enabled businesses to develop new products quickly at greatly reduced costs. This has resulted in many products having shorter life cycles, a factor that must be considered when promoting products. The key to success is the ability to identify customers' needs and then make customers aware of the new products so that they are bought. The pace of change must be taken into account when putting a promotions campaign together.

Need to know

When planning a campaign, you will need to ascertain how each of these influences will apply to your chosen business and promotional activities and adjust your plans accordingly. Equally importantly, when you are assessing the success of an existing business's promotional campaign you will need to explain how these factors may have affected the promotional activities currently being employed by the organisation. This ability to effectively analyse and evaluate both likely influences and their effects on either the past, present or future promotional activities of the business will go a long way towards ensuring that you achieve the criteria for higher grades in your portfolio work.

How to evaluate a promotional activity, page 54

The following synoptic case study draws together many of the areas previously associated with planning a promotional campaign. As you will have recognised by now, there are many different 'balls in the hand' that marketers have to juggle, representing the complex world of marketing and business. The highly competitive world of business means that no business can rest on past success or practices any more, as proven by Marks & Spencer. They must be always evaluating what they do and how they do it, and change as needed to keep up to date and ahead of the rest.

This case study looks at the changing world of marketing and covers recent changes that have great implications for promotional campaigns. The main issues being covered here are influences on promotion, setting and achieving objectives and the importance of budgets. You would do well to read the case study carefully, and if you have time, look at how these changes have affected the relative success of Procter & Gamble and Unilever since this article was written.

CASE STUDY

P&G to make adland pay

Sunny Delight's maker calls the creatives' bluff with performance-related commissions

The clock is ticking for the moody creatives of adland. Procter & Gamble, the world's biggest advertiser, whose brands range from Pampers nappies and Tide detergent to the Sunny Delight "citrus beverage", has called time on the traditional reward system and says it will only pay for results.

Although P&G says it has the support of the four advertising agencies which handle most of its £2.2bn annual budget, the switch will send a shiver round an industry which has never quite shaken off the accusation that it is a costly and largely ineffective luxury.

All the studies designed to show that advertising helps create and cement brands, to increase sales and strengthen the corporate balance sheet will now take a back seat to the hard reality that the advertising industry will increasingly be forced to put its money where its mouth is.

P&G – which is desperate to increase sales after revenues rose by only 3% last year – says it does not expect the new system of payment to have a substantial impact on its major advertising agencies yet. But the £300m of commissions they have been used to receiving each year is now expected to come in the form of a flat percentage of revenues from the company's brands.

This is designed to link the fortunes of the advertising agencies more closely with those of P&G, whose sales should, if the advertising industry's story is to be believed, reflect the strength of the ad campaigns.

There has already been a shift in advertising away from traditional above-the-line advertising. So the time-honoured 30-second daytime television slot which spawned the "soap opera" is increasingly giving way to below-the-line media such as direct mail which tends to provide greater accountability and cost effectiveness. The £9m marketing blitz by Saatchi & Saatchi which brought £160m worth of sales to Sunny Delight, together with *Marketing Magazine*'s accolade of most successful brand launch of the 1990s, is a notorious case in point.

The big consumer goods companies such as P&G and its rival
Unilever have otherwise tended to be conservative, fearing that
housewives will veer uncontrollably towards unbranded washing-up
liquids, own-label washing powders and rivals' frozen peas if a
continuous steam of reinforcement is not pumped out of their
television screens day and night.

But the winds of change were apparent when Unilever chief Naill
Fitzgerald told a gathering of advertisers earlier this year: "For 40
years in the UK, agencies' skills, reputations and profits have been
centred around, almost to the exclusion of all else, the conception
and production of 30-second spots for network TV. But there are vast
and irreversible changes taking place in the world of communications,
and not one of those changes will favour network television."

A proliferation of competing terrestrial, cable and satellite
broadcasters has dramatically diluted the audience which the main
ITV channels now deliver. A similar pattern is apparent around the
world. Demographic changes such as the sharp rise in single-person
households means different communication channels, such as the
Internet, are being explored to reach the young male audience.

Improved response measurement has given a new lease of life to
traditionally unfashionable advertising media such as billboards,
which used to be seen as suitable only for booze and fags. Now,
though, posters advertise everything from new television series to top-
of-the-range cars.

P&G's change to performance-related pay is expected to mean a
shift from traditional television and print media toward more closely
targeted outlets such as direct mail. Simon Lapthorne, media analyst
at Granville, pointed out that sophisticated agencies which already
allocate the promotional budget across several channels would
benefit from the shift. He said an agreed measurement system was
crucial, as sales can vary according to the economic cycle or other
factors outside an agency's control.

 Direct mail, page 39

Nick Phillips, director general of the Institute of Practitioners in
Advertising, yesterday claimed that agencies had little to fear from a
shift to payment for results.

"The extent of the remuneration is far more important than the method
of payment," he said. Admitting that P&G was seen as a "role model" in
the advertising world and that its move would prompt others to rethink
their strategies, Mr Phillips said: "There's a lot to be said for incentive
schemes which reward achievement, but they need to be fair."

The IPA holds awards every other year to recognise the most
effective (rather than the most attractive or best directed)
advertisements. Entries have to be supported by detailed papers
explaining the rationale and outcome of the campaigns. The IPA now
has a dossier containing 800 case studies ranging from the 1958 PG

Tips chimps campaign which was credited with helping to lift the tea brand from fourth to first position in the British market and raising its market share from 10% to 23% to the "good to talk" campaign fronted by Bob Hoskins for British Telecom.

And while spirits companies say our turn to advertising has failed to arrest the decline in tipples such as whisky, it is clear that the drinks groups which have spent less on marketing and promoting their brands have lost share to better supported rivals. The enforced inclusion of values for brands in company balance sheets since the end of last year is also expected to focus attention on the ability of advertising to build brands as well as the value which advertising can add.

But for Procter & Gamble the issue is far simpler. "Our overarching objective is to increase top line sales growth," the company said. But, if the change of advertising strategy helps P&G succeed in its target of doubling sales between 1995 and 2005, there will be a lot of smiley faces in adland.

Lisa Buckingham, *The Guardian*, Friday September 17, 1999

© Lisa Buckingham

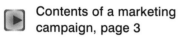 Contents of a marketing campaign, page 3

A CTIVITY

1 What are the major changes in the operation of advertising brought in by Procter & Gamble and Unilever?
2 According to the article, what effects are the movement towards performance-related pay for running campaigns likely to have on the selection of media to be used in communicating the campaign messages?
3 Why is it important to measure the success of a campaign against its cost?

I How to evaluate a promotional activity

The final stage in the process of planning and running a promotional activity/campaign is the evaluation stage. This is vital to the effective running of the campaign, and should begin even before the campaign is finished so that any corrections needed can be made as soon as possible. If the plan has been well prepared, with clear aims and SMART objectives, then the evaluation stage should not be too difficult.

SMART, page 10

Need to know

In your portfolio work, you will need to evaluate the promotion
activity of your chosen organisation. This aspect of the coursework is
vital for the higher grades and so should be completed with the same
attention to detail as the other activities. Too often candidates perform
this task with less zeal and care and limit their final grade to Ds and Es
because they fail to evaluate effectively. Although evaluation is a skill,
it can only be learned through practice, and the activities in the
following section should not be skipped over.

What areas should I be using to evaluate success?

Achievement of objectives

Ultimately, whether you are assessing an existing campaign by your
chosen organisation, or the appropriateness for success of your own
campaign, the means of evaluation are simple. At the end of the day, a
promotional activity or campaign will be deemed successful if it has
achieved all of the stated aims and objectives originally set out in the
promotion plan. The closer the results are to meeting the stated
objectives, the greater the extent of the success.

 Objectives, page 7

Need to know

Where the assessment criteria requires that you evaluate the success of
a chosen organisation's campaign and then recommend an alternative
approach to achieve the original objectives, you simply need to
concentrate on what went well and what didn't work. Your new
approach should concentrate upon using different activities to
overcome the weak areas in the campaign. Your assessment should
seek not only to identify what didn't work, but also WHY certain
activities didn't work. This should then enable you to clearly prepare a
relevant alternative.

Sales levels

Comparing planned sales levels with actual sales levels in terms of
volume of sales, value and/or percentage changes will be vital for many
activities. The degree of success will be determined by whether what was
aimed for was achieved or not, and if not, by how much the targets were
missed.

 P&G to make adland pay,
page 52

Branding, pages 33–34

Need to know

Percentage differences can often be more illuminating than simply pure figures. For instance, a promotional activity may miss the sales value target by £1 million. However, if the increase in sales planned for was £50 million, the target has only been missed by 2%, a figure that reflects a successful campaign.

Product awareness

An important indicator of the extent of success of a promotional activity or campaign is product awareness. This is measured by the percentage of the researched population who know about the product after a stated portion of time.

Need to do

- For your chosen organisation research the targets set for product awareness.
- Research how successful they were in reaching that target.

ACTIVITY

1   Why do you think so much importance is given to the assessment of product awareness?
2   What are the likely consequences for a business that fails to reach its product awareness target?

Changes in repeat sales

Many promotional activities can persuade people to try out their products, especially if the means of persuasion involve discounts. However, repeat sales are vital if a business is to establish itself and/or its products in the market. So some comparison of changes in repeat sales should be measured and evaluated when seeking to assess how effective the activity was. Unless the business is able to establish a core of loyal customers it will struggle to see medium and long-term success in its operations.

Brand loyalty

A clear indicator of a successful promotional activity is the extent to which customers are brought to the point of practising brand loyalty. This is obviously down to reinforcement tactics and is evident, as already mentioned above, in repeat buying. However, brand loyalty can also be established for businesses which have ranges of branded products or a diversification of products under the brand name. For instance, a customer may be persuaded to buy Kellogg's cornflakes by an advertising campaign. However, they may enjoy the product so much that they buy other Kellogg's products and stay loyal to the full range of cereals, not just the initial product.

Tasks

1 Identify four other brands where a range of products may be bought under the same name.

2 Using these four brand names, explain what it is about them and their promotion which cause people to be loyal to them.

Reputation of the organisation

As already mentioned, one of the most powerful means of gaining a competitive edge during the past 10 years or so has been the establishment of a strong, positive image. Communication of an organisation's social responsibility has played a big part in image development and is still seen as important in the twenty first century. Any positive improvement in an organisation's reputation should be seen in a positive light when evaluating promotional activities.

 Pressure groups, page 49

It is worth noting, however, that some promotional activities can result in negative publicity but improved sales. So care must be taken when evaluating the effects of advertising and other promotional activities on reputation, as this may have a positive overall effect on the business.

Read the following case study concerning French Connection's advertising campaigns.

CASE STUDY

French Connection plans to surprise with new TV ad campaign

Fashion group French Connection is planning a TV advertising campaign "to surprise and excite all our customers" – just a year after a TV watchdog banned its last adverts because of their "unacceptable level of innuendo".

The group's founder and chairman Stephen Marks has turned his nudge-nudge FCUK logo into an international brand with campaigns using straplines like "fcuk fashion" and the "fcukinkybugger" that the advertising authorities objected to. He is selling commemorative pre-World Cup T-shirts emblazoned with "Fcuk football". But yesterday he promised that the new ads will be "sexy and interesting ... but not rude".

Mr Marks was announcing another sparkling set of annual profits – up 21% to £23.2m before tax and goodwill. The company said the economic slowdown and the after-effects of September 11 had hit sales in the US, but Mr Marks said strong Christmas sales in Europe had offset the downturn and the US problems could provide "an opportunity to acquire interesting retail sites at sensible rentals".

This year has started well, with like-for-like UK retail sales up 5% and strong wholesale order books. "It is difficult not to be upbeat with the numbers we have produced," he said.

The group, which also owns the upmarket Nicole Farhi label and the Toast catalogue, is launching an e-commerce operation at the end of next month, when its Buy Mail mail order business, which includes the entire French Connection collection, goes online.
Mr Marks is also extending the brand with licensing agreements ranging from fcuk alcopop to fcuk shoes later this year.

Julia Finch, *The Guardian*, Wednesday March 13, 2002

© *The Guardian*

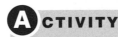 **CTIVITY**

1 Evaluate the impact of French Connection's fcuk advertising campaigns on its reputation, stating examples to support your assessment.
2 How successful were the campaigns in terms of sales and profits?
3 Should French Connection continue using the fcuk logo in its advertising campaigns? Support your views clearly.

Satisfying the target market

It goes without saying that any advertising or promotional activity must address its target market's needs in order to be successful. Failure to do so would result in a negative set of results of any of the previously stated assessment criteria. This was one of the major failings of Marks & Spencer before they brought in Luc Vandevelde as Chairman to rescue their falling sales and profits. One of the key reasons cited for their failure by Lisa Armstrong, fashion editor for *The Times* was "their failure to understand the new lives of women, their target customers for clothes and food sales."

This issue of target markets is covered in the following case study.

 Choosing the right media, page 20

CASE STUDY

Marks & Spencer boss leaves on a high note

Luc Vandevelde is to step down as chief executive of Marks & Spencer after delivering on his promise to revive the fortunes of Britain's biggest clothing retailer, it was announced today.

Mr Vandevelde, 51, who originally joined as executive chairman before taking up the chief executive role two and a half years ago, promised to turn around the store in two years. In fulfilling his pledge, the Belgian executive leaves on a high note.

But the real test of his legacy will come in the event of an economic downturn. Like other retailers, M&S has benefited from a ravenous appetite for consumer goods in the past two years and analysts will be watching to see how M&S copes in more difficult times.

 Economic factors page 44

But Mr Vandevelde undoubtedly leaves M&S in better shape than when he found it, when sales and profits were down as shoppers took their business elsewhere. Mr Vandevelde decided to focus on UK operations and sold or closed shops in continental Europe.

Stores were refurbished and new designers such as George Davies from supermarket group Asda, were brought in to freshen up the company's clothing lines. The focus on clothing paid off as M&S has reported improving sales in all adult clothing areas, with the best performance coming from womenswear, its previous weak point. Total sales in the 14 weeks to July 6 were up 9.1%, with clothing, footwear and gifts showing the biggest increase, of 14.8%. Home goods were up 5.9%, while food sales grew by 2.9%.

"We are a different and focused business today," said Mr Vandevelde.

Mark Tran, *The Guardian*, Wednesday July 10, 2002
© *The Guardian*

ACTIVITY

What indications are there in the article above that Marks and Spencer has now begun to meet its target market's needs?

Cost effectiveness

The final major area you could use to evaluate the success of a promotional activity is its cost-effectiveness. A method you may have already covered in the core marketing unit to assess this is the advertising elasticity of demand. Unless the promotion campaign is cost effective, it

 P&G to make adland pay, page 52

does not really matter what improvements you may have gained, it should be evaluated in a negative manner. Each business will have its own idea of what is cost effective. Pizza Hut, for instance, uses a formula to gauge the return on its advertising spending and for every £1 spent on advertising each branch must generate an increase of £2.35 worth of sales.

Need to do

Investigate the costs of promotional activities in your area. A useful starting point is the cost of advertising in the local newspaper and possibly the nearest commercial radio station. This will help in costing any new promotional activities you deem necessary for your evaluated organisation.

Examining board assessment evidence guidance

What follows is a detailed look at the three main examining boards for this area, namely:
- AQA: Unit 15 – Using Sales Promotion
- OCR: Unit 8 – Promoting Business Activity, and
- Edexcel: Unit 7 – Marketing and Promotional Strategy.

The information relates directly to their published specifications of assessment evidence. It is essential that you obtain your own copy of the assessment evidence sheet from your tutor.

Each Board will be dealt with separately and you will be given an indication of the type of research, information and data you will need to collect. There will also be advice on how that data should be used to ensure that the highest grade possible is achieved.

Wherever possible, the guidance will relate directly to a specific area on the assessment evidence, i.e. E1 or C4.

Due to the nature of the topic (in that it is up to you to carry out and investigate organisations and products), the guidance will be general and form an overview of what is required.

AQA: Unit 15 – Using Sales Promotion

You need to produce a proposal for a sales promotion campaign for a product or range of products of a business that you have chosen. The proposal must include:
- Background to the product or market situation.
- Objectives for promotion.

- An explanation of the type of promotion that you have chosen as appropriate.
- An explanation of other types of promotion.
- Examples of different communication materials that you could use.

Grade E

E1

You need to identify and analyse a market situation that can be improved by the use of sales promotion.

This is where careful selection and background work is essential. You need to know that you can gain access to enough information. It may be an existing product or service that you feel could be improved if it was promoted more effectively. The choice of organisation is essential.

Ensure you have information and evidence that clearly shows the current position of the product or products; this will give you a bench mark to show how your proposals will improve the situation.

E2

Identify your objectives for the sales promotion and the type of sales promotion that you are recommending.

What are you hoping to achieve? It is essential that you ensure your objectives are clear and measurable. Examples of possible objectives may be outcomes such as an increase in sales by 20% over the next six months or increased brand recognition by the under-17-year-old age group.

E3

Explain why your proposal is appropriate.

This will link closely to the objectives that you have set in E2. It must take into consideration the size and type of organisation or product that you are promoting. Take into account the cost of the promotional activities you are suggesting. Ask yourself whether it is feasible that they could budget for such a campaign? Consider the product and decide where it would be most suitably promoted and by what method. Also, don't forget who you are promoting it to. What is the make up of your consumer and how would they be best communicated to?

E4

Explain clearly the way that any constraints have affected your proposal, including legislation.

Refer to both internal and external constraints, be specific and state what the constraints are and what effect they have had. Consider the wider issues of reach and OTS as well as areas such as budget. Refer directly to the ASA and the rulings that have been made previously regarding content and overtones of advertisements.

E5

Produce a realistic proposal with examples of communication materials.

Again the emphasis is on realistic, so take into account the product, consumer and size of the business. An international television advertising campaign is achievable for Nike, but is realistically beyond the reach of Arthur Scroggins, local plumber.

Discuss clearly exactly what communication methods you intend to use and why. Give details of where and when they will be used, highlighting the benefits of your approach.

Collect examples of similar material to emphasise and back up your argument.

Grade C

C1

Show how you planned your investigation and that you used original research.

This is an excellent opportunity for you to include a plan with dates, times and outcomes in. A clear and full description of the methods of investigation, both primary and secondary, is essential.

Original research refers to the information that you have collected. Include and discuss how you collected primary data: it could be a questionnaire to ascertain the perception of a product or service. It may be the notes from an interview you have had with someone within the organisation.

It is important that you hold onto all the information that you have collected. It can always be placed in appendices in your portfolio for reference. If you do use appendices, make sure that you directly refer to them in your report and explain what aspects they hold which are relevant to your report.

C2

Summarise alternative types of sales promotion that you have not used, noting their advantages and disadvantages compared with examples from other outlets.

This needs to be more than a list if you are going to achieve this grade. Consider which types of sales promotion you could have used but didn't and comment on the reasons why you disregarded them. It may well be that they had some very good points, but in your opinion they were not appropriate. Consider also a wider number of promotional activities that you could have used but didn't: once again, using the book as reference, list their advantages and disadvantages. You can also show how alternative promotional activities have been used by other organisations and the benefits that they obtained by using them.

C3

Explain how the sales promotion that you are recommending will meet your objectives.

This directly relates to E2: we can see now why we needed the objectives to be exceptionally specific to meet these criteria. Go through each objective and put forward your case for why the promotional activity that you are suggesting will meet these objectives. Just consider the positive aspects of your suggestions and why they meet the objectives you have decided on.

C4

Identify different methods used to communicate promotion and summarise their advantages and disadvantages.

This is different to C2 as this criterion is looking for you to discuss methods of communication and not just sales promotion. Again, refer back to the book and discuss the various methods used to communicate promotions. Give examples that you are aware of or have come across that relate to these methods and suggest the advantages and disadvantages of each one.

This criterion allows you to tell the Board exactly what you know about the differing types of communication used in promotion. However, do not forget to discuss fully their advantages and disadvantages and do not limit yourself to those related to your investigation. This criterion is different to C2: ensure you do not repeat yourself. This area is looking for an overview of types of communication used in promotion.

Grade A

A1

Evaluate critically your proposal against the strategic objectives of the organisation.

Note the changes in wording: 'evaluate' asks you to look back and reflect on the work that you have done. The criterion is asking if your proposal has met or will meet the organisational objectives. This reinforces the need to collect accurate and detailed information at the beginning of your investigation. It is essential that you are realistic in what you feel your outcomes will be. Look at the organisational objectives again, and then discuss how your plan has worked to meet them.

A2

Demonstrate that your proposal is both feasible and viable.

This links closely with E5; however, you are now required to validate your work. You must take into account the organisation and its environment as well as internal and external factors. You must show that you have taken all aspects into consideration when developing your promotional plan.

A3

Show how you can evaluate and measure the effectiveness of the sales promotion you are proposing.

This is an ideal opportunity to use the book to its full extent; consider a number of the methods that have been discussed in the book and apply then to your proposal. Explain why you are using these specific measures and why they relate to the particular approach that you are adopting.

A4

Show how relevant and accurate the costings of your proposal are, particularly for method and types of sales promotion used.

If you have followed the guidance in the book you will already have this to hand, information on types and cost of media is essential. Display your work clearly, preferably in a spreadsheet. Ensure that you reference your work and that you are not plucking figures out of the air. Refer your figures to actual data collected and ensure you cover all the costs involved in your proposal.

OCR: Unit 8 – Promoting Business Activities

You need to produce: an investigation of the promotional activities of an organisation and your recommendations for alternative approaches that will meet a set of promotional objectives. This **must** include:

- an analysis of an existing promotional campaign used by the organisation
- a presentation, using the evidence from your analysis, on a proposal for an alternative promotional campaign that can be used by the same organisation
- Careful selection of the organisation is essential and an ability to have access to information and data will be a key requirement. You will be looking at what the organisation is currently doing with regard to promotion and discussing how you would change it.

Grade E

E1

Identify the promotional objectives of your chosen organisation.

What is it that the organisation is hoping to achieve by carrying out promotion; for example, is it to increase sales, awareness or market share? It is essential that you ensure your objectives are clear and measurable. You need to give as much detail as possible, as this will play a major part in achieving the higher grades.

E2

Describe the range of promotional activities used by your chosen organisation.

This criterion is still referring to your information collection. What does the organisation currently do? You must identify and describe all the various promotional methods that the organisation is currently using? Any evidence or material that you have collected, for instance brochures, articles, etc. would be extremely useful as evidence.

E3

Investigate and explain why your chosen organisation uses these particular promotional activities.

This needs to be more than your opinion. You must show thorough evidence of investigation into your chosen organisation. Written evidence or interview transcript would be ideal. Why are they using the methods they are – is it due to cost, reach, tradition, etc? You must show clearly that you have investigated the organisation through the level of specific detail included here.

E4

Identify a range of constraints and explain how these could affect the promotional activities of your chosen organisation.

Refer to the book for a detailed insight into constraints, both internal and external, which relate to your particular organisation. Show awareness of legislation and the environment that the organisation is operating in. You must also take into account factors such as size, market and customer profile.

E5

Produce and present your own proposals for an alternative approach to one identified promotional objective, using appropriate promotional activities.

Up to this point your work has been based around your investigation into the organisation; this criterion is looking for you to choose a particular objective of the organisation and put forward what you feel would be a suitable and appropriate promotional plan. You must give detail about the types of activities that you are going to use, explaining clearly why they are appropriate for the given objective, organisation and environment that the organisation operates in.

Grade C

C1

Explain how the promotional objectives support the overall aims of your organisation.

This is focusing on an area of an organisation (promotion) and asking you to show how that area supports the organisation's overall objectives. You need to look at the organisation's objectives, and identify which of those can be met or supported by the promotional objectives. You must do more than just list them, you need to explain, showing that you understand and can interpret objectives.

C2

Assess the effectiveness of the promotional activities used by your chosen organisation, measured against the promotional objectives.

This criterion allows you to focus on what the organisations is currently doing with regard to promotion and discusses how effective that is in meeting the promotional objectives. You need to deal with each promotional activity that the organisation uses in turn, and measure it against the objectives. An alternative way for you to tackle this criterion is to ask this question:

Is the organisation meeting all its promotional objectives through the promotional activities it is currently employing?

If not, which activities are failing to meet the objectives?

C3

Justify your proposals for your alternative promotional activity.

Particular reference needs to be paid to the word 'justify'; you must show that your proposal has taken into account a wide range of factors and is not based purely on what you think. It must relate to the organisation, its products or service as well as the market and environment that it is operating in. You must show clearly why your proposal is appropriate and feasible. Ensure you deal with all your proposals as outlined in E5.

Grade A

Evaluate your alternative proposal, comparing it with existing promotional activities used by your chosen organisation and justifying the approach you have identified.

In essence it is asking you to look back and reflect on what you have suggested and what the organisation is currently using. Direct comparison of activities will allow you to clearly justify, with the use of evidence, why you have chosen your particular method. This particular criterion is looking for depth and evaluation. You must consider all elements of the current promotional activity, discussing the positive and negative aspects fully as well as dealing with your own proposal.

A2

Evaluate how effectively your alternative proposal will enable the promotional objectives to be met.

Reflection is essential to meet this criterion. You need to take an overview and consider why the objectives set will be met, with support from evidence collected or referenced material. You need to consider the organisation's promotional objectives and show clearly where your proposal meets those objectives. However, to gain this grade it is not sufficient for you to merely state that your proposal will meet the objectives. You must show how effective your proposal is, will it meet them fully or will it support some other promotional activity in reaching the objective?

Edexcel: Unit 7 – Marketing and Promotional Strategy

You need to produce:

- a comparison and evaluation of two competing organisations' strategies for the promotional aspects of marketing for similar products and services, and
- a marketing promotional plan for a selected organisation's product or service. It should contain:
  - appropriate use of the marketing promotional process and associated concepts and tools
  - the application of key components from the promotional mix selected from advertising, branding, packaging, public relations, sales promotion, merchandising, direct marketing, interactive media and the Internet for an identified target market and identified objectives
  - a detailed rationale for key components that you have selected;

For success in this unit you need to choose your organisations carefully; you need to find two organisations that are operating in the same market, and ideally the same size and customer base. Your work is centred on comparing, analysing and evaluating their approaches to promotion.

The second area of this unit is the development of a promotional plan for an organisation's product or service. You must choose an organisation that you are familiar with or have good access to. You will need to obtain a great deal of information from the company to allow you to complete your portfolio fully.

Grade E

- A valid comparison of two organisations' approaches to marketing promotional strategies for a similar product or service.

This criterion requires a detailed look at how the two organisations that you have chosen promote themselves in relation to the product or services that they offer. Any material that you can collect to use as evidence will be useful. If possible, compare how they use the same medium, for instance, do they advertise in newspapers or magazines and if so which ones and why?

- Logical well-structured objectives for the promotional plan for your product and a clear identification of target group.

Your objectives should follow wherever possible the SMART approach to objectives:

- **S**pecific
- **M**easurable
- **A**chievable
- **R**ealistic
- **T**imed

You should state clearly what you hope to achieve by carrying out your promotional plan.

You should also clearly identify whom it is you are hoping to communicate your message to. Try and segment the market so that you have a clear picture of the person you are trying to engage with your promotional activities.

- Appropriate application of a promotional mix and plan to your chosen product.

Ensure your plan is appropriate; you must take into account its size, the internal and external constraints as well as the environment in which it operates. You must also ensure the promotional activity 'fits' with the organisation and the potential consumer.

- Identification of the use of the key components of the marketing promotional plan with a rationale for why you have chosen them.

This is where you need to justify your approach, it will be closely linked to the previous two criteria with regard to appropriateness and logic. You must identify the parts of the promotional plan you intend to use and state why you are using them. Ensure you relate your work to the organisation and its objectives. You can also include areas you have not chosen, stating why you felt they were inappropriate.

- Evidence of relevant research to support your ideas and your approach to the promotional mix and plan.

This will allow you to describe the method of investigation and research that you have carried out. Ensure you retain any information you collect. It can always appear in the appendices of your portfolio. You should also consider using other established approaches as a means of reference for your work.

Grade C

- Valid analysis of the two organisations' approaches to marketing promotion of a similar product or service illustrating the differing techniques used.

As opposed to just stating what the approaches are you need to analysis each company's activities. You need to consider in detail why the organisations have adopted the approach they have. (Good contacts are essential, as mentioned, in order to gain this sort of information.) Again, consider all forms of promotion that the two organisations are undertaking and consider fully the differing techniques they employ.

- That you have used the marketing promotional plan format and evaluated the areas of it showing appropriate coverage of its contents.

Close reference to the work detailed in this book will be essential to meet this criterion. You must take a very structured approach to this area; consider the work discussed in the section on 'promotional planning'. Deal and evaluate in detail each element of your plan.

- Application of the appropriate promotional mix to reach the identified target market in an integrated way.

You are required once more to justify your approach; you must state why it is appropriate in the circumstances and for the target market you are

attempting to communicate with. This is also asking you to show how
your plan will work (meaning how the various approaches you are
suggesting are aimed at a set target market), therefore all your
approaches must have the same outcome.

- Referenced research material and a creative approach to the
  formulation of your promotion recommendations.

You must show evidence of independent research. What have you
collected or found out? Based on this, your recommendations will be
developed through your interpretation of the information you have
gathered, making it personal and independent. Consider alternative
approaches other than the normal channels of promotion.

Grade A

- Competitor analysis, which indicates current use of the promotion
  process and actual use of the differing key components and analysis
  of why components have not been used.

This work must be related to the organisations you have been
investigating; it should highlight how the organisations are applying
key concepts and identify the key elements of the promotional mix
that they are employing. You should fully discuss why they are using
these concepts and attempt to evaluate the likely success of their
approach. You should also fully consider the elements they have
chosen to ignore and analyse why that might be (for instance cost,
reach, OTS, etc.)

- An integrated approach to the use of the promotional mix and that
  you can discuss in detail the practical application of key
  components which would achieve the objectives set for the
  identified target.

You must show a clear use and understanding of the concepts and tools
that you have discussed and suggested. You need to take a holistic
approach and consider all the elements together. You must show that
you understand how they will operate in a practical environment. Ensure
your work and discussion is focused around meeting the objectives set
for the identified target. State how and why your approach will work,
fully justifying it and referring to other material you have collected or
come across to back your argument up.

- Referenced external research and practical use of the tools and
  concepts of marketing promotion.

You must show that you have considered a wide varied approach to your
work; your work should be the result of much investigation and
consideration. Refer to any information collected or obtained and the
manner and relevance of that information to your promotional plan.
Your work must show an appreciation for the business environment and
that promotion does not just occur on its own. Consider the other
factors, which need to be considered when planning a promotional
campaign. Ensure you show a full appreciation for the practical as
opposed to purely theoretical outcomes of your plan.

| Key marketing and promotional terms

ABC1: Wealthy consumers (categorised according to occupation).

Brand: Name, symbol or design used to identify a specific type of product and to differentiate it from competitors' products.

Customer segmentation: Dividing up customers according to their individual or grouped characteristics rather than treating all customers alike.

Demographics: Aspects of population patterns and trends, e.g. age, sex, occupational distribution.

Focus groups: Small groups of consumers brought together to discuss their use and perceptions of products or potential products.

Market leader: The firm that has the largest share of the market, measured by sales (value or volume).

Market research: Systematic range of activities designed to find out the views and thoughts of both potential and existing users of products or service.

Life-cycle: The process through which products pass from launch to growth, and then from maturity through to decline.

Market focused: Being driven by the needs and wishes of consumers.

Market research: Systematic range of activities designed to find out the views and thoughts of both potential and existing users of products or services.

Market segment: The result of dividing up large heterogeneous markets with similar needs into smaller markets (segments), according to shared characteristics.

Marketing: Identifying, anticipating and then meeting the needs and requirements of customers.

Marketing mix: The main variables through which an organisation carries out its marketing strategy, often known as the four 'Ps', product, price, place, promotion.

Maturity: The stage in the product life cycle when there is little room for expansion because most or all of the target market is saturated.

Product portfolio: The range of products developed by an organisation.

Promotion: Making products and services better known through a range of activities.

Qualitative research: Research that reflects the opinions, views and thoughts of consumers.

Socio-economic groups: Consumer groups classified according to job and income.

| Useful website addresses

The following is a list of sites that you will find useful in completing your portfolio work.

www.thetimes100.co.uk – Case study-based site looking at leading organisations and dealing with business issues.

www.bbc.co.uk – A whole range of resources – go to the education or archive area for more detail.

www.guardian.co.uk – Centred around the newspaper of the same title – archived area with key word search is very useful.

www.nike.com – Leading marketing and promotional sportswear manufacturer, website has latest advertising campaigns to view.

www.cocacola.co.uk(.com) – Go to advertising area and view latest promotional campaigns, good background and company history.

www.bankofengland.co.uk – For background statistical and government policy information, very useful for constraints and influences, access the interest rate area for more information.

www.bized.ac.uk – Business education site that contains relevant marketing information.

www.bnet.co.uk – Business Management Information site with case studies and information.

www.mad.co.uk/mw – Online marketing magazine covering up-to-the minute marketing issues and developments.

www.oft.gov.uk – Contains advice on consumer rights, competition policy, consumer protection, and lists of OFT publications and press releases.

www.asa.org.uk – Ensuring the standards of non-broadcast advertisements in the UK. Site contains the British Codes of Advertising, research and database of adjudications on complaints.

www.cim.co.uk – Information resource for marketing and sales professionals: membership details, services, and news.

Appendix

Ⓒ ASE STUDY

Legal case: Pharmacia & Upjohn

Drug firm's TV adverts test industry rules

A drug company which has sponsored a series of television commercials to be screened this autumn is being accused of covertly advertising medicines direct to the public.

The advertising campaign, which has already begun in print and poster form, is intended to alert the thousands of people who suffer in silent embarrassment from bladder problems to the possibility of treatment, says Pharmacia and Upjohn, one of the leading UK pharmaceutical companies which manufactures a drug to treat the condition.

But critics say the campaign is a clever and calculated first step down the slope towards adverts for prescription medicines in Britain, a practice banned by law, which would increase enormously the pressure on GPs to hand out expensive new drugs to patients who had seen them hyped on television.

In the US it was the growing number of disease-awareness campaigns such as that being mounted by Pharmacia and Upjohn which led eventually to the food and drug administration allowing products to be advertised by name. The drugs bill in the US has grown by 12–14% a year since then, compared with just 5% in the UK.

The incontinence campaign features a smiling, carefree middle-aged woman, and urges those with bladder control problems to ask their doctor about treatment. It features the name and logo of the sponsoring drug company.

Already GlaxoWellcome, manufacturers of the new flu drug Relenza which could be in huge demand over the winter, and of Zyban, which helps people stop smoking, has said it will consider similar "public awareness" campaigns. Astra Zeneca has run such a campaign in France, and might consider mounting one in Britain for a migraine treatment.

Pharmacia and Upjohn's incontinence campaign is backed by the Royal College of Nursing, the Patient's Association and various patient groups, which all argue that there are thousands of people – mainly women – suffering in agonised silence from a treatable condition. "The particular campaign is a very cleverly chosen one," said John Chisholm, chairman of the GPs committee of the British Medical Association.

"I don't know whether it was their idea or there was discussion in the industry about testing the rules. A lot of people suffer and don't realise help is available.

"The question is whether this is the thin end of the wedge opening the door which other people are going to walk through with perhaps more questionable motives." David Gilbert, author of a policy report on prescription drug advertising to the public, said he did not believe the industry was a trustworthy source of impartial information. He believed the campaign was designed to push at the boundaries of what is allowed.

"The World Health Organisation's ethical criteria for drug promotion objects quite strongly to hidden or disguised promotion, which is what this is," he said. Joe Collier, professor of medicines policy at St George's hospital School of Medicine, said: "They know what they are doing is creating a concept of need and widening their market and getting access to the public with their name."

Roy Sutherwood, director of public affairs at Pharmacia and Upjohn, said the campaign had the approval of the medicines control agency, which enforces the legislation. "We found fairly widespread enthusiasm for education on this problem," he said.

He acknowledged that the relaxation of the law in the US followed such campaigns. "Direct-to-consumer advertising is a separate argument, but I think I'd want to say we can't reasonably contest the right of patients to be better informed about their treatment, and pharmaceutical companies are best placed to ensure that accurate information is given to patients wishing to know more."

Claire Rayner, of the Patient's Association, who is recording the voice-over on the television adverts, said if advertising to the public was "honest, open and clear", it should not be a problem.

Sarah Boseley, *The Guardian*, Wednesday August 18, 1999

© *The Guardian*

Index